OSC IB STUDY & REVISION GUIDE
FOR THE INTERNATIONAL BACCALAUREATE DIPLOMA PROGRAMME

OSC

167 IB Secrets

Tips, hints, and cunning tricks
for getting better IB grades

Revised Edition

UPDATED FOR
2017

FSC

Tim Williams

OSC IB Study & Revision Guides

Published by OSC Publishing,
Belsyre Court, 57 Woodstock Road,
Oxford OX2 6HJ, UK

T : +44 (0) 1865 512802
F : +44 (0) 1865 512335
E : osc@osc-ib.com
W: osc-ib.com

167 IB Secrets
Tips, hints and cunning tricks for getting better IB grades
SL & HL
© 2017 Tim Williams
9781910689394
394.01

The material in this book has been developed independently of the International Baccalaureate Organisation. OSC IB Study & Revision Guides are available in most major IB subject areas. Full details of all our current titles, prices and sample pages as well as future releases are available on our website.

Printed and bound by CPI Group (UK) Ltd, Croydon CR0 4YY
www.cpibooks.co.uk

Acknowledgements

Many thanks to Elizabeth Williams for support and imprimatur, and Violet Lindsay for early help. Enormous thanks to Supriya Chaudhary for so much work and commentary, and whom I forgive for the Mr Miyagi comparison (google 'Miyagi Karate Kid Car wax'…). Especially enormous thanks to Anna Williams for reading, encouragement, layout, and tactful advice. Yet more enormous thanks to Sue Baudoux who has saved me from myself so many times and offered such excellent advice.

That plagiarism thing? Every teacher knows that most of their best ideas emerged from working with excellent colleagues—and so I mention just as examples Liz Stephan, Andy Colley, Gautam Sen, Sally Robertson, Greg Pliska, John Hutchinson, and James Layman for their competence and generosity over years. There are dozens of others too, and probably all of them will be horrified at what I have done with their ideas.

And above all, the students, far too many to mention individually, friends (often, splendidly, still friends), and enemies who endured so much, and taught me so very much.

What Use Is This Book?

Schools, the International Baccalaureate Organization (IBO), teachers—they're worried about education. So am I, of course. But this is much less glorious—a book for students who'd really like a lot of practical help on how to get, say, six extra points on their final Diploma score.

It isn't a substitute for studying in school—it's about making the best use of that knowledge to impress examiners at the crucial moments. It's about picking up a few vital extra marks here and there in enough subjects to maybe lift you just over a few grade boundaries.

It's not magic. And while I can tell you what things you can do, I can't make you the kind of person to do them. But learning the rules of the very complex game of International Baccalaureate (IB) exams can make you a better player. Like any game, there will be different views about how to get the best results, so it's going to be sensible to listen to all the different advice and decide for yourself. And don't cheat.

Use it only from time to time, when you're starting on presentations, or commentaries, or extended essays, or whatever. If you read it all at once, you'll just forget most of it—see the section on 'Memory' to understand why you need to forget so much.

This isn't the official IBO guide to anything, although everything should fit IBO policies and rules.

Contents

© Tim Williams

An Incredible Un-secret Fact

Start with this incredible fact. Students stress about final exams—but in many cases, you'll have got half your grade *before you even get to them*. This has all kinds of effects, but has one extraordinary implication for you.

Imagine an exam system in which they *ask you* what you want to study, let *you decide* how to study, even let *you write* some of the questions.

Then they let a friend mark your work, give it back to you, tell you how to improve it, give you time to change all the mistakes, and only then does the system actually give you a grade.

What kind of lazy idiot could do badly in a system like that?

And this is the IB system—between 20 and 50% of your grades you can get from work that you can write, check, triplecheck, get friends and families to advise you, change work, mark yourself, work out (pretty certainly) what mark the examiner will give, change it again…and again…

Even more—the examiners give you exact *descriptions* of what is good work and how to get the grades.

Even more—the examiners write *advice* after every session on how to get *better* grades…

So, make the most of it—you can, literally, almost get the Diploma before you sit the final exams. Enjoy.

(Ah. Before I forget—a quick technical note to do with gendered language in this book. You and I are both aware (I hope) that teachers may be of different genders, either 'he' or 'she'. Well spotted. But I am lazy and in this book will just call them a kind of neutered 'they'. I doubt 'they' will read this, so let's not worry…)

> "Continuous assessment plus final exams—a way to ensure that students get ulcers as well as nervous breakdowns."
>
> *Derek Rowntree, Open University*

 Author's Tip

Use these margins to write notes. There are also notes pages at the rear of this book.

 Author's Tip

Get the Subject Reports. These are where the examiners explain what exactly was good or bad in last year's subjects, courses, exams, and give a whole section of advice to teachers and students on how to do better. Your teacher should have them, should have read them, and can give them to you.

Writing Good Essays Isn't So Hard

You think you know what an essay is. You *may* do.

Essays were used in China for many centuries, principally to sort out who had the ability to learn thousands of facts that were both useless and arbitrarily chosen. Then the British Empire got hold of the idea and changed it slightly, arguing that your ability to write 2,000 words of philosophy in a few hours was an obvious way to sort out which chaps aged, say, 25, would be good at running 50,000 people's lives, from sewage system engineering to tea plantations. Then some British universities which specialised in producing that kind of chap started using essays for exams. And then the IBO thought that was a good idea. That's why you do a lot of essays. Obviously.

So, do IB essays test how much you know, how good your English is, what you know about tea plantations? No. Or at least that's not their main intention.

- IB essays test whether you can give a *precise answer to a very precise question.*
- IB essays test whether you can *use evidence and logic to support that precise answer.*

Keep that in your head because it seems simple, and, in some ways, it is, but it's easy to drift away from it.

Your teachers will give you a method for writing essays. Almost any method can work. Just hang on to the idea above. *A precise answer to a precise question. With evidence and logic.*

It can be very useful to think of the process backwards, to think about where you want to end up, then how to get there. It's probably how you actually tackle the job of writing the essay. So, this is something like what you do when told to write an essay:

- Someone asks you a question—your overall answer is going to be the last paragraph or *conclusion* of the essay.
- You will have to support or prove that answer / conclusion, giving your evidence and your reasons—that will be the body of your essay which leads up to that final paragraph.
- You'll have to start by discussing a few ideas and definitions to explain yourself—that will be the *introduction* which clears the way for the body of the essay.

The Essay-writing Process

- Think what your answer is to the question.
- Think of the reasons / evidence for / proof of that answer.
- Plan the sequence of the ideas; check that they answer the question.
- Write the essay.

Your School and Essays and Well-meaning Lies

In your school, the teachers will teach you a method of writing essays. They will tell you it's the only or the best way to do it, and will demand you do it, and maybe mark you down for not doing it. This is entirely reasonable but only part of the truth.

It's the *International* Baccalaureate.. In other words, the IBO needs to accept lots of different conventions and methods for doing work in many different countries. If there *is* a single correct method for doing anything, then the IBO must say that explicitly. For essays, they don't.

Things your teachers might well say:

- Never use the word 'I'.
- Always use the word 'I'.
- Always use the passive voice.
- You must have a 'thesis sentence'.
- Don't always use a 'thesis sentence'.
- An essay has four paragraphs.
- Have a 'hook' in the first paragraph.
- Always use the mnemonic 'PEE'.
- Avoid the mnemonic 'PEE'.

All they are trying to do is get you to do one method well. Go along with it. Do one method well. Probably, almost *any* method will do as long as you're consistent throughout—and as long as it offers a precise answer to that precise question.

> "[His writing] had only one fault. It was kind of lousy."
>
> *James Thurber*

The really good essay, step by step

The introduction

This is really important. Really really really important. Examiners will tell you that they basically have a very good idea what your final mark will be after they have just read the first paragraph.

What's the point of the introduction?

In, e.g., Language A, if someone asks you, 'Do you think love is an important theme in the texts you have studied?' you're going to say which kinds of love you're going to focus on—love of country, parents, animals, sports, music, girlfriends…?

You'll want to define what you mean by 'important'—the writer said it was central, it gets talked about a lot, you liked that problem, the characters refer to it, critics picked it out…?

You'll need to say that you're going to write, e.g., just about 'Hamlet', 'Othello' and 'The Crucible'.

So, in the introduction:

- **Define any central key term you'll be using all through the essay**
- **Mention what texts / areas / periods / species you will focus on**
- **Outline / signpost the points you're going to be discussing.**

 Author's Tip

Check your first paragraph. *Never* misspell the name of a text / person / character / country, or the examiner starts off thinking that you're obviously an idiot. You may be one, of course, but you don't want them to be thinking that, especially when they'll be thinking that throughout the rest of the essay.

Different subjects have different conventions—*listen* to what your teacher tells you about what to do in the introduction, in addition to the above advice.

Very Important →

The body

This is where you discuss the three points you're trying to prove, which lead to an answer to the question. Generally, in literature and in social sciences, I have regretfully to tell you that there are probably no *right answers* that the examiner is waiting for you to produce (though there are definitely *wrong answers…*). Furthermore, the examiner probably doesn't care in the slightest about your *opinions*. That's not what you're getting marks for. Look at the Criteria.

Maybe you want to say that **1.** romantic love is a motivating force in all three plays; **2.** love of ideas influences two main characters; but **3.** unreasonable passion is more important than love in all three texts.

You could equally well argue the exact opposite. It doesn't matter. What matters is whether you can explain your ideas and whether you can find evidence to support them.

So, in the body, for each point:

- **You need to say what the point is**
- **You need to explain it**
- **You need to have evidence to support it**
- **You need to show how it helps answer the question.**

Conclusion

If you've done the previous work right, then this is simple: it's just your overall answer to the question in the final paragraph.

It's where you're essentially saying, 'Having looked at these three points, we can now see that the answer to the question is…'

So, you end up with a complex answer. However, the examiner knows how you've got there; they see your reasons; they know you have evidence for your opinion; and, they also understand you have chosen what to say out of many possibilities you were aware of.

So, in the conclusion:

- **Make sure you give an explicit answer to the question**
- **Explain / show how that answer is supported by the three points you discussed**
- **Check for mistakes**—you don't want to leave a bad impression on the examiner.

So, in the really good essay:

In the *introduction*:
- Define any central key term you'll be using all through the essay
- Mention what texts / areas / periods / species you will focus on
- Outline / signpost the points you're going to be discussing.

In the *body*, for each point:
- You need to say what the point is
- You need to explain it
- You need to have evidence to support it
- You need to show how it helps answer the question.

In the *conclusion*:
- Make sure you're got an explicit answer to the question
- Explain / show how that answer is supported by the three points you discussed
- Check for mistakes—you don't want to leave a bad impression on the examiner.

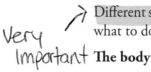

Author's Tip

Three good points is usually about right—for an essay or presentation, or commentary, whatever. *Two* points looks like you haven't many ideas; if you discuss *four* points you may not go into enough detail. Three is good.

✔ Eight tips for better than 'good' essays

*Yes **and** no.*

Examiners of course like it when you have an answer which agrees or disagrees with the question. But they much prefer it if you write about how something is, e.g., right *and* wrong, good *and* bad, true *and* not true, etc.

Assess your evidence.

If you can, try to discuss whether your evidence is reliable or not…Is there a lot of it? Can you believe the sources? Is it all from one point of view…?

Assess your sources.

You can add a short footnote to the main text highlighting what is good or bad about a particular source.

So what?

You produce your answer and then look, briefly (a short paragraph) beyond it. E.g., if love wasn't important as a theme, so what? Does that make them better or worse as texts?

Use some of the words of the original question in the final paragraph—it unconsciously reassures the examiner that you've stuck to the question.

Other points of view.

Have you thought about what the question might be like for people from other cultures?

In some ways I agree, in others, not.

Not quite the same idea as 'Yes and No'. A good essay will often finish by saying 'So in some ways the answer might be…but in other ways….'.

Pre-emptive strikes.

Point out and discuss the limitations or problems in your ideas and arguments—before the examiner stops to think about them.

> **"Thank you for your essay. I'll waste no time in reading it."**
>
> *Anon*

[handwritten note:] ⭐ really try and use these tips some maybe silly but they work !!!

There are presentations in a lot of the courses

Presentations

"Speeches are like babies—easy to conceive but hard to deliver."

Pat O'Malley

There are a lot of IB marks involved in presentations: in Language A, Language B, Theory of Knowledge (TOK), Group 4 Project…

Presenting is a set of skills you must *learn*—organising ideas, finding vivid ways to show them, controlling panic, doing several things at once, reacting to strangers' reactions to what you say and do…Learning not to finish by saying 'So—any questions?' and the audience all start looking at the desks, and there's this long silence, and then the teacher takes pity…

Here are some preliminary bits of advice that will help:

- If you're actually *interested* in the topic then you'll do better research; you'll be more lively talking about it; you'll be able to discuss it better. See the advice on choosing a topic in the section in this book on Extended Essays—anything can become a suitable topic (if not too rude…)

- If you're thinking about college applications, then the topic can become a useful sentence in a college application essay to demonstrate interest in a subject

- Try using the five cunning trick TOK questions—see the section on TOK—or look at the Subject Guide (ask your teacher if you can borrow a copy). They often suggest starting points

- If you're really stuck, try presenting against some point of view—if you can't think of something you're interested in, you might find it easier to attack or criticise something

- Read the Criteria: they are different for different kinds of presentations. For each thing examiners want to see, write yourself a sentence describing how it will emerge and be seen in your presentation. E.g., if it demands 'connection to real life situations…', how exactly will you make sure your teacher sees, hears, and understands what that connection is—so they will give you the mark?

The nine steps to a good presentation

Beginning, **Middle**, and **End**. Ok, yadda yadda yadda, you know this. But it's more complicated than you think.

The beginning

The hook.

It's great to start with some puzzle, some question, some problem, a teaser, that the audience want to find an answer to, and your presentation promises an answer by the end. Maybe, 'Do you think the universe is infinite? I'll prove it's not.' Or, 'What does belly-dancing have to do with hurricanes?'. Or, 'Most of Shakespeare's audience was bisexual—does that matter?'

A signpost.

Think of when you're learning a foreign language and you listen to a conversation—it's a lot easier to follow if you have an idea what the topic is. Same for presentations or lessons—if someone tells you what it will be about, you can follow much better. So, you say, 'I'm going to argue x, y, z…'. Or, 'First, a skit, then a quiz, then a talk—and you have to work out the connection.' Or, 'Raj will talk *for X*; Mariko will argue *against*; I'll argue it's *irrelevant*.'

WIIFM. (What's In It For Me?)

In other words, you need to give your audience a reason to listen—what's the connection with them and their lives? Maybe, 'If we knew how big the universe is, we'd have faster Internet.' Or, 'We can predict which of *you* will have sideways or head-on accidents when you start to drive.' Or, 'Ryan will show how weather balloons affect your IB grade…'

The Middle

These are the points which are the heart of what you're about, what you want to consider, or get your audience to think about. When you're preparing, try to put each point in a very clear single sentence. *Imagine* putting it up on a PowerPoint slide—would they understand it?

Look at your ideas from different points of view. Consider using the TOK questions. Or maybe have someone in your group arguing against them. What are the *problems with* or *arguments against* what you're saying?

Show the transitions between each point. You can just tell them, or have a different speaker, or move to a different place, or start presenting in a different format, or…

 Author's Tip

Vary your method of presenting for each point. Students in audiences usually start to drift off after 2–3 minutes.

The End

This is almost the most important part. It's what is in the teacher's mind when they give you the mark. You need to:

- *Wrap it up:* make sure the audience got the points you were making, and give them a conclusion, so they see what the purpose of what you were saying was, and why it mattered

- *Open it up:* give the audience ways to express their opinions or argue. This needs thinking about; e.g., get them to vote, or make a choice in groups, or talk to each other

- *Take out the hook:* give them the answer to whatever the hook was, if it isn't now obvious: 'So that's why belly dancing leads to a hurricane.' Or, 'Now you see why even the universe isn't infinite.' Or, 'I won't ask for a show of hands, but you see now why bisexuality was important for Shakespeare's audience.'

How to present

A simple rule: think of *not* talking. Think of it as a series of images, pictures, diagrams, models, maps, graphs, actions, events, film clips, activities, games—these carry and show all the *information* and *content*. What you and your group might do is talk about them, comment, and explain connections and implications.

 Author's Tip

It's really helpful to plan your presentation in a story board—what will it *look* like? This will help to stop you just chatting nervously.

Using *visuals* also stops the audience looking at you. More interesting for them, less panic-making for you.

┌ IBO allows groups (2 ppl good)

Work with one or two others if you can. More than that and someone is always sick on the day, or lazy. On your own is hard. Make sure you can describe what each of you individually has actually done to get separate grades.

Use the Criteria for that kind of presentation

Just read the Criteria. Read them. If you haven't got them, get them from your teacher. READ THEM Remember: they're all that any examiner has, including your teacher. You just get marks sooooo important! according to what the Criteria say. Read 'How Do I Get Inside an Examiner's Head?' (you should have an later in this book. idea of your grade before you present)

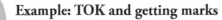

Big Author's Tip

See the Tip in the box below? Do that list of sentences for *any* presentation that gets marked, in languages, or science, or arts, or whatever. Just get the Criteria and read them, and list what you need to be *seen* to be doing.

Author's Tip

Start your preparations by writing a sentence which describes each of those things bullet-pointed on the left.

Author's Tip

Ask your teacher, in *class*, in *public*, what has made presentations successful in previous years. Do they have videos or samples you can look at?

Author's Tip

Check the practical stuff on the day, before school starts. It's awful to watch when a group haven't got the photocopies, or don't know how to work the projector, or don't know who speaks next…

Example: TOK and getting marks

If the TOK Criteria says, 'Identified a Knowledge question relevant to a real-life situation', then you need two things to get the 5 marks. Take a wild guess—what are the two things? This isn't difficult…

1. You explicitly identify a 'knowledge question'.
2. You explicitly identify a 'real-life situation'.

Here's a partial list of things your TOK teacher needs to see that you do, so they can give you the marks. It can even be worth throwing in a sentence in your presentations saying exactly and explicitly that you are now doing these things. If you don't know what those things mean, go ask your teacher.

- Explain the 'Knowledge question'.
- Connect it to a 'Real life situation'.
- Show 'Personal involvement'.
- Explain 'Why the topic is significant'.
- Show how there may be 'Different perspectives' on the topic.
- Show how your point of view is 'connected to different areas of knowledge'.

Those were for TOK. You have *different* Criteria for Language A, Language B, Group 4, and so forth, so you need to make sure you do specifically what those Criteria demand. Get them from your teacher; work as a group to turn them into bullet points; check your teacher will see the points being covered.

Use your teacher

Get them on your side. Involve them. They usually chose to be a teacher because they *want* to help. Usually. Of course, they may hate you. But if you checked with them about everything in advance, they can't really mark you down afterwards. Do all your thinking; get it together; and, a week before you're due to present, ask your teacher nicely if you can talk with them for 5 minutes. One of your group should ask about the following:

- *Check your topic.* Your teacher can't tell you what to do. But if you say, 'We're going to do this, and this, and that—does that seem workable?' They can offer an opinion.
- *Check it fits the Criteria.* Does your proposed presentation cover the things you're meant to do? E.g., run through that list of sentences bullet-pointed on the previous page of this book.
- *Check the format.* Explain how many minutes you're going to present, how many people, the method…
- *Check the practical things.* Can you set up in the classroom in advance? Will there be a projector? Can you re-arrange the chairs if you put them back afterwards? Can you use a photocopier…?
- *Killer question:* 'If you were us, what single thing do you think we could do to improve our proposed presentation?'

Preparing for your presentation:

- Practise your presentation two times. You'll be less nervous, twitchy, inclined to say, 'err, umm, ah'. You'll get the practical problems sorted out (Who starts speaking when? Who starts the projector? Who answers the questions?)
- Practise, at least once, swapping round the jobs of speaker / technician / actors / etc., so you'll be able to carry on if somebody is missing on the day.
- **Do one practice in front of a friend, or family (or maybe better, video yourselves practising in the space you're going to be using) and ask them to use the criteria to grade you. It's amazing how accurate they can be, and now you'll know what to improve.**

How Not to Speak in Public

Everyone has some problems speaking to groups of people. I've worked with successful professional actors who quiver and whimper before they go on stage, singers who have to take Valium so they can perform, and very experienced teachers who jitter and bounce around the classroom. Here are the typical problems and how to deal with them.

The biggest problem is generalised nervousness. A recent survey suggested that the thought of public speaking was more immediately worrying for most people than the thought of death.

- *Panic, nerves, meltdown*…Learn to control your breathing. A very simple method before you speak: breathe in on the count of four; hold it for the count of four; breathe *right* out for four; hold it for four. Do these four times. Try it—it works. Much more, and more specific, advice on this issue is in the section 'Panic, Nerves, Fear'.

- *Twitchy, don't know what to do with your hands, arm waving*…Write your notes on a stack of *numbered* note cards, and hold them in both hands.

- *Avoiding eye contact.* Divide the audience into three sections in your mind—left, right, and centre. Look at each *block* in turn—that way, you're not having to decide who to look at and for how long. In extreme cases, get a friend to sit in each block and look at them—that way, people feel they've been more or less looked at! Get your friends to nod encouragingly…

- *Speaking too quietly.* Ask a friend to sit in the most distant point of your audience, and just pitch your voice so they can hear you. Everyone else will automatically hear; you won't need to SHOUT.

- *Saying umm, ahh, like, you know*…A biggie. Everyone does this (listen to your teachers). Practise your presentation in front of a gang of middle school brats who mimic you exactly every time you say one of those things.

- Blanking out, not knowing what comes next…Have that stack of note cards. Or put a BIG poster of main points on the desk or the back wall of the room. Make sure your partners know what should come next so they could cover for you.

'"Why are we going in here, daddy?" "Shut up," he explained.'

Ring Lardner

 Author's Tip

'Me? I don't have no problems…' Yes, you have. *Video* yourself practising the presentation in front of people who aren't your friends (try middle school brats). Look for:

- jittering
- waving hands
- speaking too fast
- hesitations
- pausing to look at notes
- panicking eyes
- umm, err, like, aaaaand, you know, yah…

How to Cheat and Lie, Generally

How to cheat

There are many ways of cheating. In fact, the IBO includes them as just one aspect of malpractice which also includes things like:

- Having a mobile phone in the exam
- Talking about exams within 24 hours of taking them, to someone outside your immediate school community
- Using unauthorised calculators
- Impersonating other students
- Fabricating data in experiments
- Unauthorised materials in exam rooms
- *Many* more things.

> To find out what the IBO says about coursework, malpractice, and plagiarism, look at this link:
>
> **http://handbooks.ibo.org/exist/ rest/app/pub.**
>
> Many of the ideas in this section are dependent on the information available on the IBO's public access website at:
>
> **http://www.ibo.org/**
>
> The most useful part of the IBO website for students is:
>
> **http://www.ibo.org/information for/students/**

In practice that means things like using your older sister's coursework essays, using chunks of stuff downloaded from the internet, writing furtive notes on your fingernails or legs to use in exams, fiddling your data just a bit for coursework…

Or using one of these ridiculously dim websites for example:

http://www.courseworkbank.info/

http://www.angelfire.com/wizard/ib-notes/

http://coursework-writing.co.uk/ib_coursework

http://golookatthetipboxtotheleft.

The IBO's method of dealing with these is simple: more or less a blunt hammer to the head. If you're shown to have used them, you fail the whole Diploma. Oops.

How to plagiarise

Plagiarism is the act of using another person's words or ideas without giving credit to that person, and the IBO gets very, very irritated by it.

In fact, I theoretically could have just failed the entire IB Diploma and wasted two years of my life *right there*. That's how irritated they get. Because the first half of that sentence was taken from Webster's Online Dictionary, and I didn't say so. Two years wasted for using 16 words.

And worse, it's not just using someone's *words*—it could be their ideas. Well. Well. I don't know about you, but most of my ideas came from someone else—I don't even know where they came from. Unfair? Yes. Hard to understand? It can get that way.

Author's Tip

Of course, you're now going to check out these websites on the right if you didn't already know them. *BUT WAIT*. It's an *examiner* who *knows them* and is telling you about them. These websites generally are absolutely *toxic*—using them is like juggling chainsaws. Use your brain for just 12 seconds: who uploaded the materials and why? Who wrote them? Who graded them? Why are they there? Were they plagiarised in the first place? Who's scamming whom…?

So:

IF YOU ARE IN ANY DOUBT AT ALL, GIVE A REFERENCE.

IF YOU ARE IN ANY DOUBT AT ALL, GIVE A REFERENCE.

Oh, hang on, just think about this:

IF YOU ARE IN ANY DOUBT AT ALL, GIVE A REFERENCE.

It's really that simple. Nobody will give you a hard time about having too many references. In fact, it will probably move your grade up.

How to lie

You may well *want* to lie about your homework, your absence, your sources, who did which work, where you went last night…Well, there are several ways that people show they're lying. Teachers may not be able to *tell* you these, but they often know them unconsciously. These signals below come in clusters:

- Touching the ears
- Touching the nose
- Pulling on the collar (telling lies makes you feel warmer)
- Rubbing just below the eye (see Bill Clinton in testimony to Congress…)
- Blinking the eyes more frequently
- Smaller eye pupils
- Looking up to the right
- Covering the mouth
- Trying obviously to suppress all these movements.

Notice it's not usually the words they use that show someone is lying—you can practise those after all…Successful lying will take a lot of practice—you have to learn to control these unconscious reflexes, then you have to make the lie so believable that it might as well be true, and then you have to spend a lot of time and energy remembering which lies you told.

I used to tell students that they were very welcome to lie about why they hadn't done their homework, as long as they made it more interesting and believable than the truth… They'd smile, then look confused, then look thoughtful, then go away…After that, it became just an entertaining game.

How to be an idiot

The point is this: the IBO is composed of people who spend their entire days working with exam students. Between the *tens of thousands* of teachers, parents, administrators, examiners—all of whom were once students themselves—who have worked for the IBO for *decades on end*, they *know* the tricks. They actively investigate all those wonderful magic websites. And remember, I'm an examiner, and I could tell you a dozen forms of malpractice you never even thought of—and I know them and *you* don't. Hmmm. You do not know more than all these tens of thousands of people put together.

(Wait till you see a roomful of examiners hooting with laughter at an Extended Essay, where some poor sad 17-year-old has tried to convince them that they wrote something really clever.)

Author's Tip

Having some primary sources—people you have spoken to personally in the course of your research—is likely to impress examiners a lot.

Author's Tip

Other students, friends and family members also have brains and may have given you ideas—it is absolutely reasonable to attribute those as 'personal communication'.

Money Tip

This is a long-term saving idea from Supriya: using or copying other people's ideas and words without permission is called breaking copyright and is theft, and you can get sued for it. Learn now to avoid a life of crime… Start by not copying this book, continue by always attributing all ideas.

Author's Tip

Have serious, full-on bibliographies—you can cite all the texts you read, textbooks, articles, websites, conversations, personal communications, teachers, dictionaries…

Author's Tip

Remember your bibliography only contains the sources that you have used, that you have referred to in your writing. *Not* everything you ever read on a subject.

Author's Tip

Annotate your sources—write a quick footnote for the ones you use a lot, assessing their value; e.g. 'An excellent general introduction, short on data', 'clearly biased article', 'Chapter 7 a useful survey', etc.

How do you give yourself away?

- Changes in the quality of your ideas
- Changes in the style of your language
- Recognisable ideas
- Recognisable data
- Making a really stupid mistake in the middle of very good work
- Writing something excellent in the middle of mediocre work
- Your supervisor asks you a question about your work that you can't answer
- Your school gets the same examiner again and he recognises work
- Getting the right answer from the wrong data.

I was told about somebody who got away with cheating…

Right. Always there are rumours, legends, gossip flying around about who did what, who got away with what, how some student, somewhere, who was a friend of someone, did this or that…But oddly, it's hardly ever someone that you personally know…

Of course, the law of averages suggests sooner or later someone writing an Extended Essay, for example, will fool their supervisor, *and* the examiner, *and* the senior examiner, *and* the committee that looks at suspect work. But fail to fool even *one* of those and you end up with a lifelong problem with your reputation—for the sake of *maybe* one point?

If you're the kind of idiot who wants to cheat, probably no reasonable argument is going to persuade you not to. But believe me? In the end, it's less hassle just to do the work.

How to Deal with Low Grades

Serious, serious question. Can you answer this deceptively simple question below? *Do not read anything past this* until you have answered it. If you do skip this, maybe that's part of why you get low grades…

> In three phrases only: what three *practical* things do you need to do to improve your grade in your worst subject?
>
> 1. Study new material before class
> 2. ask questions – All of them
> 3. practice questions + study more frequently

The number of students who look bewildered here is horrible. It's just as much the teacher's failure as the student's, but it's the student's problem. You have to know what you need to do to improve. Knowing *how* to do that is a problem, but you can solve that.

The IB is in many ways a very predictable and boring examination system. It has to be. It's trying to examine tens of thousands of students from dozens of wildly different cultures and societies. So everything you need to do and know is written down somewhere—there are no secrets. You can find out exactly what is needed for success…

The IB describes exactly what good or bad work is in any part of every subject so any examiner or teacher—or student—in the world any time should be able to grade all student work the same way and give the same grades. Does it work perfectly? Of course not. But the Assessment Criteria are a very good start. Get hold of a copy of the Criteria from your teacher. They're not secret!

Go through the Criteria and check you understand what everything says. Do this with a friend so you can share understanding. Well. Potentially anyway. Identify all the different skills. Highlight them. *Do you know what you are meant to do?*

Okay. You really ought to end up with a list of things you now know you need to work on for any given subject. If you can't do this, well, tough luck. Give up. Nobody can help you. There are no Fairy Godmothers for Grades. But you really ought to end up with a list. It might be something like:

Example 1: Language A
1. How to write the introduction to an essay.
2. How to use evidence to support an idea.
3. How to take apart a poem for a formal commentary.

Example 2: Language B
1. Constant spelling mistakes.
2. Accurate use of the past perfect tense.
3. Fluency in speech and conversation.

 Author's Tip

That question to the left? Now also ask your teacher in that subject to say what three practical things you need to do to improve. See if they can do that for you. See if you agree or understand.

 Author's Tip

Ask your teacher if they are using the Assessment Criteria to mark your work. They may not do in IB1 (in case it's too depressing for you…), but really should do in IB2. Then ask them for a copy of the Criteria.

 Author's Tip

It is an interesting fact that students (especially working in groups) can mark almost as accurately as experienced examiners. So give your work to another student and ask them to grade it—and then explain to you what you did right or wrong.

 Really Big Author's Tip

Give another student your work to grade, using the Criteria, *before* you hand it in to your teacher—then *change* the things they said you did badly. *Then* hand it in to the teacher.

Example 3: Biology

1. Answering multiple choice questions.
2. Remembering complex processes like the Krebs cycle.
3. Three basic chemical reactions in biochemistry.

Now you can get help with getting it right. Ask other students. Tackle the section in the textbook. Use a different textbook. Use a revision guide. Look it up online. Get a tutor. Amazingly—ask your teacher?

Should I give up?

If you *really*:

- Have used the Assessment Criteria
- Can identify *why* you're getting low grades
- Have tried to get help with identified issues
- Are *working* on those specific issues
- And still can't get better grades…

Well, you're like I was with Maths. Useless. But actually, that's not such a *big* problem. Remember that you can get between 20 and 50% of your grade in class, and *that* is something you can work really hard on. If you manage to get even half marks in internally assessed work, then you probably only need to get another 20% in the final exam to get at least a 4 overall.

Make sure you get the best possible grades for all your coursework. Use your friends, your family, your teachers, a tutor, work-mates, the Criteria, revision guides, online tutorials… Spend time and energy on it.

Identify what you can do in that subject—and really, really work on those so you can get as many marks as possible in the exam.

Prioritise. How much does it really matter if you get a 3 in this subject? Is it worth losing marks elsewhere, or not?

Really plan a solid revision programme. See all the advice in '4. Exam work'.

Try a revision course just before the exam—they can help quite a lot. See the Author's Tip opposite.

Overload and Burn-out

A year is 365 days—but not if you're doing the IB. It takes about 20 minutes to work a weird kind of magic spell and reduce a year to very little time. A major problem is that your teachers probably don't talk much to each other, so they all (6 or 7 of them) merrily set deadlines and workloads independently. That leads to sudden surges in how much you have to do, so you get tired, fed up, fall behind. It's tough, and frankly nobody much cares (maybe your Granny cares?). Welcome to the world.

What you don't need is to let it get away from you. You need to see the problem, and, if necessary, be able to *show* the problem to somebody else (and not just think and talk about it). If you're going to try and negotiate solutions, you can't just say 'Ummm—I think I have too much work to do—like, help?'

1. **Get an Academic Year Calendar.**
   Your IB Co-ordinator may have a copy. Or you can download them from a million sites (e.g. at osc-ib.com, or 'templates' in Microsoft Works).

2. **Get Highlighters, Pencils, Pens.**
   Some students will have these—probably in a pencil case. Others will *always* have to borrow them. Very strange.

3. **Mark the Holidays.**
   Look at your school calendar, and highlight each and every day of all the holidays, starting on the first evening and going through to the last evening. Use a pale colour like yellow. You'll see why soon.

4. **Mark the Days You Won't Work Outside Class Time.**
   Using a highlighter, maybe blue, mark the days you're going away. E.g., holidays, ski-days, sports trips (ah—whoops—maybe a lot…), the first days of the holidays (ah—yellow plus blue highlighter—green days), CAS workdays, Christmas Day, New Year's Day, Eid, Hanukkah, Diwali, the days between Christmas and New Year, theatre performances, concerts, exhibitions. And the days after those—you won't work. Maybe you'll pretend you'll work on the plane / train / bus to… But will you? Really?

 Author's Tip

Don't lie. You're not going to work on Friday evening. And probably not Saturday morning either.

5. **Write in Your IB Deadlines.**
   Use pencil. These deadlines you may need to get from your IB Co-ordinator, or from your teachers. Don't forget IAOP, oral commentaries, TOK essays and presentations, coursework, portfolios, the Group 4 Project, performances, CAS, Extended Essay, Internal Assessments… Ah—and maybe final Exams…?! Don't forget school deadlines for these may be different from what the IB gives.

6. **Write in School Events.**
   Use pencil. Look at the School Calendar. Have you got festivals, parent conferences, visits, graduation days, college fairs, university application deadlines, school exams, expeditions, teacher training days, end of term events, half days, celebrations…? Will you really work these days? So, highlight those as you did for step 4.

7. **Count the Days and Lessons and Deadlines Left.**
   Take a deep breath first. As a guide, one very typical IB2 student discovered her 'Second Year' was actually 108 working school days, 34 IB Deadlines, 90+ schoolwork deadlines, 35+ school events and activities, college applications, mock exams, and revision on top of all that.

8. Look on the Bright Side.

There may be only 75, or even fewer, of your least favourite lessons left. (Hmm—to cover half the course?!).

9. Look on the Dark Side.

You probably haven't included everything. There may be some things your teacher didn't even know about. Do you actually know how much of the course is left to cover? Maybe your grandparents come to visit, your dog gets sick, school closes for snow or revolutions, you get ill—and, there will be days you just can't be *bothered*…

10. Do Something About It.

I'm willing to bet that 80% of your problems come from procrastination, and from your teachers not talking with each other or to you. Some of the problems may come if you're one of those perfectionists who want to keep working on everything endlessly. More and more problems come from online distraction. These are all *controllable*.

These are some of the things you can do

Talk to your teachers about problems—negotiate deadlines. Look at the section 'Manage Your Teacher' later in this book

Plan your work around the calendar—find out what's needed and set targets.

Sit down with someone else—like your parents, another student, a teacher, a counsellor—and a list of your workload and the calendar, and sort through it with them. It's amazing how someone else can help you plan / prioritise.

Sign up for a Revision Course, so that your revision is one less thing to organise or worry about.

Start working with work-mates to reduce workloads—see the section 'Work with Other Students' later in this book. Start by seeing if you can find ways to collaborate on a single job that is really stressing you. Just do that one job. If it helps, then try another.

Procrastination. Look at the section later in this book, '16 possible ways to deal with procrastination'.

Take up Zen. See the section later in this book on 'Panic, Nerves, Fear' for advice on how to deal with stress. Full-time Zen may be an over-reaction, but there are several easy things you can do. Try them.

In the space below, write two lists: one list of things that are *important* ('Need to finish EE bibliography' and one list of things that are *urgent* ('Must prepare for test tomorrow'). Highlight anything which is in both lists, start with that, do one of those jobs a day till they've gone away.

Important	Urgent

The Extended Essay

Come on, your school told you all about it—you just weren't listening…

Oh, all right. It's an independent research project. You decide what you're interested in investigating; you produce a very precise Research Question (RQ); you go out and do all the research; and, then, you write up your answer in the form of an essay. There are very clear restrictions on the *form* of that essay. It's meant to be a major piece of work, and you do it over a long period of time—usually during about eight months or so, from midway through IB1 to early on in IB2. You get *support* from a supervisor, almost always a teacher at your school, but you're meant to do it all yourself.

Your school will tell you all about it, but some of what they say will be economical with the truth. For example, they'll tell you that it should take about 40 hours of work—that is not the general experience…Each school is likely to invent its own stories, priorities, deadlines—it's wise to stick with what your school says, just because it's a waste of limited energy trying to buck the systems…

What are you interested in?

Before you read anything else here, take two minutes and just write down five things you are *actually* interested in, that you *actually* spend your free time on, that you *actually* want to know more about—video games, chocolate, travel in India, hot air balloons, how to get rich, science fiction, Taoism, spaniels, masks, calculus, cooking, puzzles—whatever, whatever…

1. _____

_____

2. _____

_____

3. _____

_____

4. _____

_____

5. _____

_____

Author's Tip

Think of possible topics *as early as you can*, even if it's just a general idea. You'll have more chance of getting a supervisor you want, more chance to change your mind, and more time to do preliminary research.

Author's Tip

Read the *subject specific* notes in the Assessment Criteria for the subject you're thinking of studying—the examiners explain exactly what they want to see in any given subject, and the subjects require different things.

How to choose a topic

What are you actually *interested* in? Did you make that list of five things above? Do it now.

What might you be interested in studying at *college*? The Extended Essay can be a way to demonstrate interest—or to discover you're not actually interested.

Can you make a *local connection*? The more local you make your topic, the more likely you are to become the world's leading expert on it. There are millions of people who know about butterflies, tens of thousands who know about Italian butterflies, and a handful who know about butterflies in one small village in Calabria.

Choosing the *subject:* FAQ

Does it have to be in a subject I study?

No, but it's much better if it is, and schools often rightly insist on it. If you don't study psychology, you'd have to study all about it to do an 'Extended Essay' in it—far too much work.

Does it have to be in one of my HL subjects?

No.

Does it have to be in a subject I want to study at college?

No, but your college application may need to explain why, for example, you want to study Physics but spent a year on an Extended Essay in Mandarin B…Note: it can actually impress colleges, if you have a good reason you can explain. Saying you didn't like your Physics teacher won't hack it…

Does it matter whether I'm actually interested in the topic?

Yes and no. If you want to do *well*, then something shines through in an essay when the student is really gripped by it, and examiners respond well to that. But if you are just doing the *minimum* to get the *points*, choose an easy topic and do it quite well.

Should I choose the IB subject first, and then look for a topic?

I'd suggest not. Any topic can be tweaked to fit one of your six subjects. See the examples below.

- **You want to study hot air balloons?**
  That could be Physics (gasses), Language A (stories about), History (first flights), Economics (of safari tourism), Visual Arts (design motifs). Etc.
- **You want to study Eminem?**
  That could be Language A (semantic shifts), Business Management (case study of), Physics (staging problems), Language B (translation to Mandarin), Music (well—maybe…). Etc.

How to use your *supervisor*

For most teachers in most schools, being an Extended Essay supervisor is unpaid extra work. They have lots of classes, marking, meetings, preparation, tutoring, training, extra-curricular activities, trips—and now, extra unpaid work? Appreciate whatever they do for you—buy them chocolates.

Remember a supervisor's job is to *support* your research and writing, *monitor* to make sure you don't cheat, and offer *comments*. In this case they are *not* your teacher. In practice, they can choose how much to help. It is *not* their job to make sure you get the Extended Essay done.

Author's Tip

Learn how not to waste their time. Understanding the research and writing is all about *your* initiative. Ask very specific questions, meet deadlines, and warn them if you are running late (see the section 'Manage Your Teacher'). An irritated supervisor is not a helpful person. A sympathetic supervisor can save you a lot of precious time.

Good supervisors have a reputation and get a full workload quickly. If you really want a particular supervisor, try asking them brief questions about your ideas *before* the school even starts the official process, get them interested, and show you're going to be a good student.

How to create the Research Question (RQ)

It doesn't have to be a question (e.g., it can be an investigation or a hypothesis), but it's good, at least, to start with one. Because that automatically gives you a structure to all the research and writing—a *question* you discuss in the introduction, that you *examine* in the body, and that you *answer* in the conclusion.

A good way to test a RQ: can you 'answer' it in one sentence?

- This will help you check what subject it should fit into. E.g.:

  'Why did Shakespeare write Hamlet?'

  'For money' (Business Management)

  'To develop revenge tragedies' (Language A)

  'The king wanted it' (History)

- It will also help you see if it *can* be answered—and therefore investigated. E.g.:

  'Do goldfish enjoy swimming?' (Bad—they may do, but how to investigate that?)

  'Do goldfish like swimming in warm water?' (Better—you could at least do an experiment. But how will you know what goldfish 'like'?)

  'At what water temperature do Belgian pet goldfish live longest?' You can see how that experiment would work, and you can get an answer (but watch for ethical issues—that's what supervisors are for, right there…You can't kill goldfish for higher grades…)

Remember: RQs are often best if they're *local, specific, answerable…*

Example 1

First idea: When do butterflies mate?

Develop more detail: When do butterflies mate in China?

Local, specific, answerable: When do butterflies mate in North-East Shanghai compared to South-West Shanghai?

Example 2

First idea: What do children think God looks like?

Develop more detail: Do children in an international school all draw God the same way?

Local, specific, answerable: Is there more variation in the ways that children from an international school draw God, compared to children from a single Spanish village?

Example 3

First idea: Do masks affect their wearers?

Develop more detail: Do European masks change the way people behave?

Local, specific, answerable: Do the masked dancers of the Binche carnival report different feelings or behaviour when they wear their masks?

Big Author's Tip

If you choose a topic that's very specific, very local, you'll probably end up knowing something the examiner—or a university admissions tutor—doesn't know. They *like* that. It's impressive to be a 17 year-old student who can teach them something…

Author's Tip

For bibliographies, use Moodle, or a small notebook, or a bookmarks sub list. Or all of them. *And* back up in the Cloud somewhere.

Author's Tip

Read the section in this book on '16 possible ways to deal with procrastination'. Do it now?

How to *work* on the Extended Essay

Okay, this is a really short section—you'll all be working on different things in different ways so there's no one-size-fits-all advice here, but there are some generally useful practical things you can do that will actually make life easier in the end:

From a group of former Extended Essay students—the three best things to do:

1. Outline what it is you need to research or prove before you start—otherwise you spend a lot of time doing general reading and not knowing if it will be useful.
2. Get a calendar and plan when you will expect to work—it's probably going to take most of a year, and some things are time-bound, like when you can set up experiments, or meet some people, or visit a site.
3. Start your bibliography on Day 1 and *always* add *everything* to it—it's easy to take things out, but hard to remember where you found an idea. And it's one job less to do at the end.

And advice from an examiner:

1. Don't be afraid to make your topic more and more limited—better to do something small very well than a huge general topic.
2. Re-read the Assessment Criteria every two months. If you haven't got them, get them from your teacher. They are vital. (Gautam thinks this should be in red capital letters…)
3. Try explaining your ideas to your granny—if she can't understand, maybe they're not clear in your own mind. And maybe your eventual audience will not understand either.

How to start actually *writing* the Extended Essay

One student started referring to the writing of her Extended Essay as 'The Monster'. Easy to understand. If you are not careful you get to the autumn of IB2 and you have this mass of notes / information / ideas piled up, and somehow you have to turn it into something of the right length etc. But you also have a mass of other urgent work, and it's really tempting to let this job go to the bottom of the pile. How could you avoid putting off the monster job forever?

- Go back to the outline you started with. Remember what your main points are, make a short list of just one sentence for each point in order.
- Don't think of writing a general draft of the whole essay—just produce a detailed *plan*. Even a non-detailed plan. You can do that quickly.
- Discuss the plan for 10 minutes with your supervisor or a friend. Is it clear what you need to write?
- Write a draft version, or even a bullet point plan, of just the *conclusion*. Will you be able to prove or support the things you say there?
- Slice and dice the monster. It shouldn't be too hard to write the conclusion. Then maybe the introduction. Then one main point of the body. Then another. Then the third. Then proofread. And check the bibliography. You're done (well—almost…).

> **Controversial idea: writing drafts is a waste of time**
>
> Some experienced teachers froth at the mouth when I say this. But really, I mean, any student who thinks they're going to have to re-write 4,000 words three times is probably going to be put off the job.
>
> So, write a *detailed* plan. It's very easy to change bullet points or a spider diagram, you can get it done quickly in any form that makes sense to you, you get to know what exactly you need to write before you start, it's easier to see the mistakes, you can discuss it easily with other people to get comments.
>
> Then write the final version, once (Okay, maybe also later—you need to make small revisions).
>
> But if you write something thinking, 'This is a draft,' then, of course, you don't do it well (because 'It's just a draft'), and you have to write the *whole thing* at least twice. And remember how much time you are meant to be spending on the EE in total? (40 hours…ho ho…)

How to *finish* the Extended Essay, and get the marks

Getting the marks

You want the grades—then get the Assessment Criteria. Actually, if you can, get your supervisor to get you a document from the Online Curriculum Centre called 'Unpacking the Criteria'. If they don't know what you are asking them for, harass them—they *should* know.

There are five Criteria and they are explained in very concrete detail. It says things like:

'Is the topic explained in terms of context and why it's worth studying?'

'Is the Research Question clearly stated?'

'Is it a maximum of 4,000 words because otherwise the student loses marks on all Criteria?'

'Is there a critical evaluation of the arguments presented?'

'Is it laid out the way the Guide says it should be?'

It's not rocket science—a lot of it could be reduced to a Yes / No question checklist. There used to be several available on the internet, often for Economics, but usable for almost any subject.

And the next thing is to make sure you have checked it against the Subject Specific Guidance—well, of course, you did that when your supervisor told you to, right at the beginning, no? But do it again before you submit it.

The only tricky Criterion is 'Engagement' and that is mostly ticked off by having kept up your Reflection Space, got to meetings at the right time, responded to your supervisor's advice (and wrote about how you responded…), and having a cracking final interview just before your supervisor writes their comments.

You can get most of the marks in an Extended Essay just by following the Guide. I could get a pass in Chemistry and know *nothing* about it. Remember: it's mostly teaching you about what *research* is, not about a subject.

 Author's Tip

Pre-emptive strikes. In the conclusion, discuss something that went wrong with your work or investigation. The examiner probably noticed anyway, and this way you look good for doing what good researchers should do (hmm—don't go on and on about problems—a paragraph will do …)

 Author's Tip

Annotate your bibliography. Once you've produced your bibliography for the Extended Essay, according to whatever conventions you usually use in your school, add a phrase which assesses the main references; e.g., 'A useful general introduction.' 'Obviously biased to a conservative view.' 'Very dubious factual bases.' 'Interesting but very dated.'

 Author's Tip

Too many words? Can you turn any of the information into diagrams or pictures or graphs? With *captions*, of course.

CAS: More Than Bake Sales, Art, and Studs

Almost certainly your school has talked or is going to talk to you—at leeeength—about CAS. No point in repeating all the stuff about how it will make you a better person, and how many hours it will take to make you a better person, and why. Etc. At the end of it, two simple facts:

- You have to do it.
- It can seriously be the best thing you do at school. Or unbelievably irritating.

If you *hate* the whole idea of CAS, if you think it's 'extra' to what you should do at school, if you just want to get your head down and solve maths problems forever or only do experiments or get stuck into Big Books, well, that's not unreasonable. There's no reason why one form of education should fit everybody.

Or you may be *hanging in* at school by your fingernails, hating every minute, trying to get by on the absolute minimum until you can get to the real world, and CAS looks like another huge lump thrown on top of everything else. I know that feeling.

Or you don't really see the *point* of it all, but if someone just tells you what to do you'll just get it done and keep everyone happy with the minimum of fuss, and get it over with. And then maybe they'll all just leave you alone so you can party.

Or you're thinking it's *brilliant*, you can do all the things out of class time that you enjoy, and get credit for doing them, get support for working with other people, do practically anything you want, and your college application will make you look like Mother Teresa.

You can make CAS what you want it to be. So:

1. Work out what you are actually interested in. Forget about whether you think it's good for CAS or not—what would you spend time doing if you could? Write them here:

   _____

   _____

   _____

2. Think about what you want to do once you've left school, or what you want to do in college. Think about skills as well as subjects; e.g., working with people, research in science, use maths every day, learn and use languages, look after money…?

   _____

   _____

   _____

3. Start brainstorming with friends, or family, or sympathetic teachers. Think of five ways you could be looking after money for school groups; five ways to use your languages in or outside school; five kinds of research that might be useful…

   _____

   _____

   _____

Author's Tip

Get there first. Even if you don't get what you wanted, the Co-ordinator will remember you as someone keen and organised, and be more inclined to help with other choices you make later on.

Author's Tip

Get there first. If you go see the CAS Co-ordinator in the first week, you'll probably get first choice of whatever organised activities may be available.

Author's Tip

Get there first. If you come up with pro-active suggestions for what you want to do in the first week of the course, the Co-ordinator should think you're great and want to encourage other students by agreeing to whatever you want.

Author's Tip

Get there first. You really *don't* want a huge backlog of CAS in IB2.

CAS can work for anybody. Really. Here are four classic CAS-hating types (of course, you're not one of these…) but, just as examples, here is what they could do for CAS…

You're an utter party animal? Design a portfolio of party decors to show art colleges; join a salsa class; run parties for school fundraising.

You only love maths? Use fractals programmes to create artwork; do statistics for the local athletics club; teach problem-solving in the elementary school.

Black metal leather? Teach a face painting and make-up unit for Middle School art class; do aerobics to the sound of ummm your favourite band (?!); develop bio-degradable graffiti methods for local gangs.

Just too cool for school? Run a fundraising fashion show; get your snowboarding certificate; create a contemporary drugs education unit that's actually realistic.

Probably your school also offers a variety of organised activities to help you fulfil CAS requirements. There won't be enough for everybody; many of them will be things you hate or which the school has just produced to soak up all the useless students. Use what you can, but think beyond.

The CAS Co-ordinator's job is usually a monster—say 40 students in each of 2 classes, each of those 80 students doing 5–8 different activities in maybe four different places, most of them getting it wrong or not doing it or asking for help every week…Read the section on 'Manage Your Teacher', work out a sensible-looking suggestion, and they'll almost certainly just tell you to get on with it. And use the tips on the right of this text.

 Author's Tip

Look at how the requirements for CAS are described in the booklet. *Use* those words to describe how your proposed activity is going to do those things—it saves the Co-ordinator having to think about it.

 Author's Tip

Write a half page proposal for the activity you want to do, give it to the Co-ordinator, make an *appointment* to talk about it for *five* minutes. (Tip: Include two problems you can imagine with your idea—and solutions for them…impress in your Portfolio…)

 Author's Tip

Never miss a deadline. It's such a pain for the Co-ordinator to chase you. *Either* just write up what you can, and add a line saying you'll write more next week; *or*, if desperate, go to the Co-ordinator two days *beforehand* and explain the problem. Just never make them chase you.

Creativity: Getting...Umm...Like...Creative About It?

This shouldn't be difficult to do. You don't need to be Leonardo da Vinci. In many places, you'll have fantastic access to activities run by museums, evening classes, art centres, theatres, clubs, colleges...Just go along and the creativity thing is practically organised and done for you.

It may not seem so obvious if you don't speak the language, or your school is five hours from the nearest cinema or tea shop. Then you'll need to look around your community or school itself. But any of these jobs below could be / involve creative activities. In school:

- Cooks
- Doodlers
- Gardeners
- Exhibitors
- Carpenters
- Window-dressers

- Phone films
- Lighting design
- Book layout
- Publicity design
- Origami makers
- Curator.

Three Creative Activities for the Uncreative

1. **Design Portfolios.** Even the words sound arty and serious. You want to be a vet—design stables. A businessman—design products. An engineer—design low-cost local housing. A scientist—design instruments. A lawyer—design offices.

   A good solid researched notebook / collection / portfolio of sketches, small projects, layouts, collages, photos, and so forth, will help you understand the subject, fulfil your CAS requirements, and look very good to colleges.

2. **Exhibitions.** If you can't create much yourself, put on exhibitions of other people's work round school. E.g. art classes, theatre designers, great maths portfolios, successful Group 4 posters, people's doodles (surprisingly fascinating if you get collections...), masks decorated and auctioned for charity, secretaries' choices of pictures, the school gardener's favourite flowers, photo-essay competitions...

3. **Classrooms.** Call it 'Creating Learning Environments.' Teachers are generally soooo lazy about their classrooms (notice they're always 'their' classrooms, not the students?). Offer to design or maintain them—try out background music, artwork, arrange plants or flowers, old rugs, a sofa, get new posters, make a graffiti wall, rearrange the furniture, make the place beautiful / exciting / surprising / relaxing / stimulating...If nothing else, you can guarantee they'll be delighted if you take on making something striking out of those awful notice boards that have the same work on them for months...

Action: No Mud, No Studs

Some students, and some schools, interpret this as meaning sports (preferably competitive, probably in gangs, even better if they involve mud, studs, and bruises). Well, no. Also see:

- Hang gliding
- Snowboarding
- Cycling
- Long-distance walking
- Building
- Meditation
- Yoga
- Tai Chi
- Tree planting
- Roller blading
- Climbing
- Dancing—of all kinds.

The biggest problem for many of these is that they're individual, often untaught, and quite possibly you'd hate to have a 'supervisor'. So, proving you've done them can be a hassle. Try the Tips opposite to make your Action more credible or acceptable.

 Author's Tip

Take the Portfolio to the Co-ordinator after a few weeks and say anxiously, 'I just want to check all this is okay?' In their mind, you get established as serious, organised, and getting on with it.

 Author's Tip

Forming a group always looks more impressive and credible: 'Member of The Friday Runners Club' sounds better than 'I go jogging, honest.', and 'The All Star Salsa Sisters Ensemble' is better than 'I like to go, like, dancing sometimes, yah?'

Service: Beyond the Bake Sales

This is what gives most trouble to most students. And schools. (It's startling just how *outraged* some people get if you suggest it's perhaps a rather unclear concept, maybe left over from days of the British Empire / muscular Christianity / missionary leadership? Maybe it doesn't help the world very much to go and build walls in Africa when the locals can do it better, you're taking their job, and, good lord, what could they have done with the money you spent getting there…?)

It all gets mixed up with a feeling that service should involve interacting personally with other ('poor') people because it will make you a better person; that you need to see the effects of what you do on some physical person; that you have to be uncomfortable in some way; that it should cost you somehow…oh, lots of things. Often people seem to be confusing two things: the *process* of service, which they think is somehow meant to make *you* a better person; and the *product* of service, which is meant to make the *world* a better place for other people to live in.

Oh, but never mind all that ranting—what can you do in your 'acting locally'?

Think carefully about what 'local' might mean. It's usually taken to mean the place surrounding your school (excellent for many reasons) but maybe also:

- In your school
- In the community of parents / workers / suppliers which revolves around the school
- In the community that you go (home) to in the vacations
- In the worldwide International School community
- In the community you spend most time with, which is quite possibly an online community.

Think carefully about what you can offer. You may think that *running idiot software to set up basic websites* is trivially simple—but you could do it for:

- School clubs
- School trips
- Local charities
- Local clubs
- Events
- You could set up a small company to offer it as a service to anyone
- Set up a social enterprise which gives its profits to good causes…

You can speak English, and another language or three. Imagine you go to a country where they only speak a language you don't know—what would you need help with? So do immigrants or refugees near you need translations, accompanying to deal with government offices, help filling in forms, buying tickets?

You can walk, read, write? There are people who can't—what can you do for them?

You have a computer, a bike, a phone, a garden, books, tools—within a few kilometres of you there are people who don't have them and could really use them—how can you share?

Five ways to use your computer for service

Warning: your CAS Co-ordinator may be rather conservative, or not adjusted to the last 20 years of change. Check with them *before you start* about doing some of the things below.

1. Let the keyboard connect you

You can actually work from home—try searching online for ways you can do something useful online. Or for ways to find interesting local organisations.

http://www.helpfromhome.org/

Part of giant searchable portal for volunteering of all kinds; this page has links to what you can do in one / five / ten / thirty minutes—now known as 'microvolunteering'.

http://www.sparked.com/

A site with hundreds of one-off actions you can take online—matches interests and skills.

2. Saving the universe, one computer at a time

There are now hundreds of projects that rely on you volunteering your computer to be used by projects that use its spare capacity when you don't need it. They are doing medical research, astronomy, psychology, etc. This is really low-key involvement and you're going to have to do something more than just volunteering your own computer…So, start a campaign in your school and community, persuading 100 people to join in—with their computers:

http://www.gridrepublic.org

Volunteer your computer to search for aliens, measure climate warming, develop clean water sources, new drugs for malaria. Simple, brilliant.

3. Saints, or black brigade anarchists—online activism

Anyone who thinks that sitting at a keyboard can't produce radical change in the physical world has clearly been brain-dead for the last few years…In fact, you could argue that to advocate serious change in the real world now without using social media or online tools is just a little naive. So, use your keyboard.

http://www.change.org/about

Change.org is an online activism platform for social change that raises awareness about important causes and connects people to opportunities for powerful action. 'We work with more than 1,000 of the largest nonprofits in the world, have a team of hundreds of journalists and organisers that span the globe, and empower millions of people each month to…' The site also offers ready-made campaigning tools, e.g., a format to run online petitions, to use for any cause.

http://ifwerantheworld.com/

Great social collaboration site—you type in what you think you'd like to change in the world, and it hooks you up with people to work on 'action platforms'.

4. Service—the computer game…

If you understand things like MMO, or MMORPG, or iOS, or Raspberry Pi, or Infinite Monkeys… then maybe you can get to bleeding edge *education*. Produce an online game for students anywhere—in your elementary section, in third world countries, in hospitals…to help them learn to read, to focus, to take their mind off pain, to write code themselves…

The giant games company Unity is giving away free game software so students can develop their own games for educational purposes (and / or make money…). Works across platforms, and on old machines found in developing countries. Great opportunity.

5. Whilst you're at it…

Whilst you're using your keyboard for anything at all on the internet, you might as well do something useful as a side-effect. Use a charity like **rtu.org** as a starting page on everyclick.com. Or play games online and raise money….Maybe these aren't *great* commitments or projects if it's just you that does them—so, start a campaign getting *100* people to do them in your community.

(continued)

> **Five ways to use your computer for service** (continued)
>
> http://www.everyclick.com/rtu
>
> Every time you start a search from here a child in India gets helpwith their education. And it takes you no effort whatsoever.
>
> http://freerice.com/
>
> Improve your vocab, maths, and general knowledge. And feed people…
>
> http://www.clickforchange.com/
>
> Play games online. And raise money for a good cause…

Portfolio

So, you have to have this. It can be a real pain. The easiest way to manage it is to write a very little very often. A sentence at a time every time you think of it will add up with no effort. Writing a full page after a month is just another extra job. So, one photo and a caption—done. A sentence. A weblink. A doodle. Lots of tiny items.

And a checklist—do you know what the portfolio is meant to be demonstrating? Is it doing exactly (just?) those things? Give the checklist to others as a service activity…?)

Interviews

See the Tips on getting there first. Frankly, a lot of research has been done on how grades are dependent on impression management, and CAS is so nebulous that it's even truer. Spend ten minutes *preparing* a really good spiel for your interview—lots of specific details, dates, places, aims; use the keywords and objectives from the Guide; have your three next steps ready to describe; press all the right buttons. Your CAS Co-ordinator will love you for five minutes and send you away happy.

> "It's not just by chance that men only get an hour for lunch break—any longer and you'd have to keep re-training them."
>
> *Unattributed*

Theory of Knowledge: Cunning Tricks. And More

TOK is meant to be at the centre of all your IB work. It's sad how it so often gets reduced to being just 'another (extra) subject'. But we're not going to fight that problem here— so you just get a few quick tricks which could help you get through it better—which I guess means with better grades…Everything below applies to essays and to presentations— they're just different ways of examining many of the same skills.

(Read the sections on presentations and essays in '1. Coursework'.)

The Five Big Tricks

1. Nothing's Black and White.

Things could be Black or White, right? Or maybe Grey. Or striped. Or Black *then* White. Or another colour completely. Or…

Same with Right or Wrong. Things could be sometimes Right, sometimes Wrong. Or Right in one situation, Wrong in another. Or neither Right nor Wrong. Or Neutral. Or Right a long time ago, but Wrong now. Or…

Yes or No? Or Yes sometimes. Or it used to be Yes but…Or Yes if certain conditions apply. Or No to you, but Yes to someone else. Or Yes to part of it, No to other parts. Or…

2. Where or who does the idea come from?

Hopefully, if I tell you something about the IB, you're going to believe me—I've got a long track record of IB work, the book's published by a reputable company, much of it fits what your teachers say, etc. It seems a credible source.

What some anonymous guy on a new student website says about the IB has to be considered carefully—who really are they, what do they know, why are they posting or uploading, do they know what they're talking about?

Same for any source—examine and assess them, and discuss them in your essay or writing.

3. What would an Esquimau say?

We tend, unsurprisingly, to think within a framework—and the IBO / international school framework tends to be very heavily European middle-class academic and rewards that kind of thinking (and oh, if you knew how upset some people get when this idea gets floated…).

But what would other kinds of people say about the topic you are studying? If you come from a culture without books, how interesting would a TOK textbook be? If you're struggling just to survive, what would be your response to a TOK question about morality?

If you were from a culture where, generally speaking, there was no grass and your lifestyle depended on killing things, would you have the same immediate responses to life as someone who's a vegetarian in an industrial society?

So—what are your prejudices (prejudice: judgements made without conscious thought…)? What do you assume is true, without really thinking about it? Being richer is better; it's right to give money away; science is important; happiness is essential; you need a career…?

Author's Tip

What's said here is probably true for essays or similar in other subjects, especially Language A and History.

Author's Tip

TOK examiners love these kinds of distinctions in analyses, and in essay conclusions. In fact, you probably can't get top marks without them. Never agree completely with a question.

Author's Tip

TOK examiners love you to talk about your sources and discuss how reliable they are. It's one of the indicators of top level work—not just excellent referencing / citation / bibliographies, but *assessment* or *evaluation* of how reliable they are.

Author's Tip

Examiners love it even more when you at least indicate that there might be several points of view, even if you have no space to discuss them all in detail…

Author's Tip

TOK examiners love it when you write I say things like 'Part of why I think *XYZ* is because I grew up in such and such a society.' Or 'I think *X* is usually better than *Y*, but maybe that comes from my religious / cultural / social background…'

(And *don't* get all politically correct on me—it was just an example. I only say Esquimau because the IBO statistical bulletin indicates that there were no Language A Inuit or Greenlandic candidates last year.)

4. Definition. Definition. Definition.

What I said above about European academics? The IBO is still caught up in a framework of thinking that is unconsciously prejudiced towards the ideas of people like Ayer and Wittgenstein (oh, just believe me—or go look them up) who believed that we can really only think about things if we have words for them. And so, the more exactly and precisely we can use words, the better we can think.

It may be Right, or Wrong (or of course, Right in some ways and Wrong in others…) but it's certainly very, very, very helpful as an idea when writing essays. In fact, a really clear definition of a key term in a question can almost answer the question by itself.

For example: 'Is love a universal human phenomenon?' Well, it depends how you define 'love', no? Love could mean a passionate interest in something, or sexual desire, or an abstract concept, or affection, or patriotism, or … Some of those are clearly not universal (e.g., lots of people don't have a country…). So, once you've decided on which definition you're going to use, the essay almost writes itself.

5. Pre-emptive strikes.

You may have noticed this by now in your life—not everybody agrees with you all the time. That may include examiners. Actually, examiners aren't paid to have opinions about your beliefs. But they do get paid to look closely at your *logic*, at how you *support* your ideas, at your *reasons* and your *evidence*.

Start thinking—if someone reads what I wrote, how would they argue with me? What kind of differences would we have? How might they say I was being unreasonable, or had no evidence? Start *anticipating* how people would disagree with you.

So, e.g., if you're an atheist and scientist, and that's important for your argument, *discuss* in your essay / presentations what a religious person would say when arguing with you. If you're very religious, consider and discuss what a humanist would say. Present and discuss opposing points of view.

Author's Tip

This issue of 'definition' is probably true for any essays, especially Language A and History and Economics. Oh. Am I repeating myself here? Must be important then.

Author's Tip

TOK examiners love students who define key terms the first time they use them, often (not mechanically always) in the introductory discussion in the first paragraph.

Author's Tip

TOK examiners love it when you write about several points of view, and when you point out the *problems* with your own ideas—what may not be justified, what may be a prejudice, what you have had to miss out, what counter arguments exist…

You've been through endless years and years of education, maybe several schools, but things are (should be…) a bit different when you start the IBDP, in how you study, deal with other students, and deal with teachers.

Yes, teachers are no longer the Mussolini wannabes that ruin your evenings; now they're your colleagues. So, you can't carry on blaming them for everything that went wrong with that last piece of work (though they will probably continue to take credit for anything you ever do right…). Succeeding in the IB requires *both* of you to do a good job. So, here are a few ways to encourage your teacher to be most useful…

Manage your teacher

Manage arguments

Suggest solutions, don't just describe problems.	
Bad	'I can't meet the deadline, I have too much work.'
Good	'I can give you the plan by the deadline, skip the draft, and give you the finished work a day late— is that ok?'
Bad	'You're so slow marking our work.'
Good	'Could you guarantee a three-day turn-around for marking if the whole class meets the deadline for handing in work?'
Bad	'We all got lousy marks for the presentations.'
Good	'Could we spend ten minutes in our next class identifying the biggest problems we have, and then you give us five ways to solve them?'

Involve them; ask what they suggest.	
Bad	'It's not fair—you're giving us an essay on top of our Maths and Group 4 Project.'
Good	'Next week we have Maths projects, Group 4 Projects, and your essay—what do you suggest we could do to manage that?'
Bad	'You give me low grades. I really, really hate you.'
Good	'I'm not getting good grades, am I? Can you suggest three specific things for me to do to improve?'

Identify agreements; isolate disagreements.	
Bad	'She's always, like, picking on me.'
Good	'I'm on time for classes, my work's in on time, I think I contribute well in class; so can you tell me if there are any problems I'm not conscious of?'

Manage your teacher's classroom behaviour

Students tend to think they are in lessons to suffer passively. They just get through class time. But even the worst classes and teachers can be made better. If it's just you that does the things suggested below, you're going to look slightly mad. But if as a *group* you try them, they can have a real effect within weeks.

- When you understand something—just nod slightly. Teachers often just go on explaining until they get some evidence you understand—and on…and on…
- When something is even slightly more enjoyable—smile a bit. Teachers will gradually, unconsciously learn to do what gets approval.
- Ask for particular lessons on particular topics—even (or especially?) if you know they are coming up anyway. It motivates the teacher…
- Especially in revision periods, go to class with a specific question prepared, needing a five minute answer. It produces more focused, useful lessons.
- Read the section later in this book on 'My Teacher Hates Me / I Hate My Teacher'.

Manage information and workloads

It may not be a Mussolini situation, but the teacher still generally has control because they control the information, and the deadlines. Unfortunately, their priorities may not be yours. You can negotiate better if you have full information. Say very politely to them that you're trying to plan your workload, so could you please get from them:

- A rough outline of what units / topics / texts the semester's work will cover
- How many major pieces of homework etc. will be asked for
- Some idea of what, if any, IB coursework will be due.

And if you're at all serious about getting good grades:

- The appropriate Assessment Criteria

And if you're really serious about grades:

- The Subject Report in the subject (or the teacher's summary of that Report)

For Subject Reports, see the box on the next page.

 Author's Tip

Bad teachers (who are not to be confused with dislikeable teachers) do exist.

You can help them get better by asking for this information in the text on the right. E.g., they may not have even thought of planning the whole semester's work, or not looked at the Subject Reports.

Keep asking them, very politely...

 Author's Tip

Get a planner and read and follow the section in this book on planning. It makes a difference.

Subject Reports

Every year, all the examiners write thousands of reports on what they saw students do in the work they marked. All these are read and summarised by the senior examiners. Then the summaries get sent to schools and teachers to help them teach better. You can read them. Every year. In every subject. Pages and pages of practical advice on how to get better grades. Read them. Each one says 20–40 things like:

- **In Physics:** 'Remember you're not penalised for incorrect answers. Make sure you practise for questions on electromagnetic induction. It's more important to study descriptions and explanations of physical phenomena than work on calculations and derivations. You cannot skip topics in revision—they *all* get examined.' And more…

- **In Business Management:** 'In quantitative questions you'll lose marks if you don't show the working. Students aren't using the correct subject terminology, so they lose marks. If you're asked for three features, you'll probably need to write three sentences I paragraphs.' And more…

- **In Maths Studies:** 'Know the difference between sketching and drawing a graph. You lose marks if you don't give the required degree of accuracy. Don't cross out working unless you replace it. Include the raw data in your project in an appendix or as part of the task.' And more…

How to use them

It would be hard to read every Subject Report in every subject you study, so here are some ways to use them:

- Split them among friends to summarise in bullet points

- Just read the sections of recommendations'

- Ask your teacher to summarise them for you…

- Ask your teacher in class to explain anything you don't understand about the recommendations.

 Money Tip

Summarise the Subject Reports—then sell the summaries to next year's students.

> **Author's Tip**
>
> *Attribute!* And that may well now include ideas you got from your work-mates. As in, e.g., 'E. Jiwnani. Personal communication, Madrid, 2012'. Or 'The author gratefully acknowledges contributions made by A. M. Hansen, C. J. Neilsen, and P. Q. Y. Peiro in developing the arguments in this essay.'

Work with Other Students

Is there any point working with others? The advantages are pretty obvious. If you work with a couple of other students (and maybe they *shouldn't* be your *friends*—see the next section) then you can:

- Generate new ideas more easily
- Explain things to each other
- Test each other
- Grade each other's coursework
- Divide revision workloads
- Work together on presentations
- Enforce work schedules for each other

The problem tends to be that fine line between collaboration and freeloading or cheating, and different schools and cultures draw that line at different points. The best thing is actually to discuss with a teacher how you are *proposing* to work on some project or coursework or whatever. *Before* you start.

A good general principle is to make sure you're giving as much to your fellow students as you're getting—so if they do a lot this time, you have to do more next time. That makes it more likely to be collaboration.

And a very important principle—if you work together on a piece of coursework, in the end you will get assessed separately. So you will need to be able to *report* and *describe* what each of you does *individually*.

Who should I work with?

- *Not your best friends.* It's easier to work with your closest friends but not the best idea. You know you'll likely end up just being social / complaining about teachers / gossiping / playing GTA.
- *Not the prom king or queen wannabe.* Just, not.
- *Not the same people all the time for all subjects.* You'll learn more from new people and their working styles.
- *You actually may want to work with the (other) quiet people,* preferably ones who obviously have been paying attention in class. Preferably if they get pretty good grades. A good sign if they have big school bags. People you have talked to in the past, but hardly know.
- *If you're in your first year,* you could choose one project to work on (like a practice TOK presentation) and just go talk to a couple of people about working together on an idea that *you propose*. You'd like it if someone said to *you* that you seemed like the kind of person who'd be good to work with and gave you a starting idea as well—so will they.
- *If you're in your second year,* you might suggest working on *revising* a particular topic just for three sessions. If it works, carry on. If not, it's not been a high risk…

Advice from (other students') bitter experience

- *Work at school* (if you possibly can). Much easier to arrange, less time spent getting your parents to drive you, more likely actually to do it, no TV / games / coffee / pool to distract.
- *Work for deliberately limited sessions.* If you know you just have 20 minutes to do something, it's much more likely you'll all just get on with it.

> **Author's Tip**
>
> Teachers are actually very happy (and surprised) to see you working together quietly in their *classroom* after school and may even help.

- *Short projects to start.* Say 'Let's meet twice, and produce note-cards on the unit on Acids and Bases' or 'Let's brainstorm ideas for three of the TOK essays.'
- *Get a bit nasty.* If someone misses a session, be a bit horrible. It's good for them (helps them see they're useless…) and for you (therapy). And it means you may both / all actually in future stick to a schedule of studying and get it done (unlike working on your own and just having a *really* quick look at Facebook…).

Author's Tip

Fix times for several sessions in advance. So they don't get shuffled / forgotten / overtaken by football practice. And so you can plan what you'll study.

Work-mates. What can you do with…someone else…?

Many things are more fun and more productive if you do them with someone else, no? Here are examples of the kinds of things you can work on together:

Essays:

- Develop 'for' and 'against' ideas.
- Brainstorm examples and case studies.
- Share research—both the work and the results.
- Point out each other's prejudices (TOK: 'Knower's perspective').
- Identify 'counterclaims'.
- Define words used in the question.
- Grade a partner's work by the relevant criteria.
- Give feedback and identify ways to improve.

Presentations:

- Divide up the jobs—see section on 'Presentations'.
- Brainstorm ideas for topics.
- Argue *against* everything, then swap round.
- TOK: Describe each of these for your presentation in one sentence to each other (you *do* know why these are important, don't you?):
    - o the 'knowledge questions'
    - o your 'knower's perspective'
    - o the 'sequence of your argument'
    - o the 'real life situation'.
- Be a practice audience, and listen to your partners presenting. Laugh if / as appropriate.
- Video each other in practices.
- Grade partners' work by the relevant criteria.
- Give feedback, identify ways to improve.

Revision:

- Make note cards to copy and share.
- Explain concepts to each other.
- Summarise Examiners' Reports.
- Get past papers to look at.
- Identify problems you both / all have, to ask teachers about.
- Write summary posters of units / topics on a big piece of paper, copy them and exchange copies.
- Test each other on the definitions in science syllabuses.
- Write post-its to put round your houses.
- Learn two quotations per exam text per session and test each other.
- Test each other on understanding the Assessment Criteria.

Author's Tip

When discussing what seem like lousy ideas, break the ideas up into parts—there's usually something good you can say about part of it.

Author's Tip

Get a calendar. Strike off all the days you *can't* work on a project, the days you *can't* meet, the lessons when you *can't* get work done. See how much time you really have. Guess how many meetings you need. Schedule them— and stick to the schedule.

When you *have* to work with others (e.g. Group 4 Project...)

Don't say 'Yes, but...' *Do* say 'Yes, *and*...'

Build on ideas—try not to reject an idea until you have a better idea to offer.

Don't just 'have a meeting'. Be clear what you have to achieve in a meeting. Teachers are *useless* at this in staff meetings—they forget if they're sharing information, getting ideas, making a decision, producing a plan...

Plan backwards from your deadline. Remember: you're not just working on what you feel like...There's an external world to deal with. See the Tip opposite.

Checklist: Probably any group project will require at least the following in addition to your jobs in the actual presentation:

- A manager—someone whom you all choose, to keep it all together.
- A recorder—who makes notes of what you decided or need to remember.
- A technician—if you are going to use *any* equipment—copiers, beamers, chairs.
- A criteria supervisor—someone who keeps checking how what you're doing is fitting the Assessment Criteria.

Deal with Lousy Handwriting

It's not surprising—you spend two years handing in all your work by email, writing coursework on computers, texting, printing everything—and then suddenly you're expected to spend hours on end in the exam fiddling with this liquid stuff coming out of a stick in your hand…

And when you get to college you'll probably never handwrite again, nor in a job, and probably the IB itself will change in a few years' time. But not for you. You need a quick fix. You do. You do not want examiners hating you. Read the section on why examiners hate you (Chapter 4)—handwriting matters in exams.

Well, but…

The trouble is that writing is like walking—have you ever tried to change the way you walk? They're both just complex, inter-connected sets of muscular habits, learnt and over-learnt millions of times a year for 17 years. You don't really, actually, *know* how you do them. So, either you have to start learning all over again from the beginning, or you have to try some moderately helpful quick fixes (and some prayers…).

Quick fixes

Dump the ball point pen / bic / biro.

Imagine a man balancing on a plank that's on a big ball. Every time he makes any move, the whole thing starts to wobble, and the ball starts to shoot off in random directions. The man is always working hard at it, he gets exhausted, it's harder to control, the ball is sliding away all the time…That's a good way to imagine what's happening when you write with a ball-point pen. It's just hard to control, and there's a vicious spiral as your hand therefore gets more tired, so it's harder to control, etc. Etc.

Get a fountain pen, with a slightly wider nib.

Imagine the same man is on ice-skates. Now when he wobbles the skates can only go in two directions. It's easier to learn to control; your hand doesn't get so tired. Like ice-skating, it's painful and unnatural to begin, but you soon get the hang of it. A fountain pen with a wide nib forces you to write BIG…Sloooow…r.o.u.n.d…

And / or get a triangular pen.

Most pens have a smooth, round barrel—and they slip and rotate so you have to grip them harder (especially if your hands get hot and sweaty, like in a warm IB exam room in May for example…). A triangular grip is much less tiring and also helps you put your fingers in the correct position. You could buy a pen like this, or you can maybe buy a grip which you can slip onto your favourite pen.

Write BIG, ROUND, SLOW.

Even if it looks like a 12-year-old's love-letters, big round writing is so much easier to read than a fast scrawl. Accept this fact—if you write ten pages the examiner can't read, it was pointless, so write half as much as usual. A wide fountain pen nib means your letters will be bigger than half the space between the lines on the paper. Good. Consciously write r…o…u…n…d…

Always put three sheets of paper underneath the one you write on.

Go back to that image of a man on a ball, and imagine now the ball is on a sheet of ice: every slip gets exaggerated at high speed. That's like writing with a biro on a hard plastic or wooden desk top. So, put three sheets of paper underneath the one you're writing on—it's like balancing on that ball on a duvet—much, much easier to control.

Make sure you get the correct angle for your wrist.

Your hand / wrist / forearm need to form more or less a straight line going vertically up and down the page (you can angle the page on the desk if you need to). Once you start bending your wrist, or your arm starts going *across* the page, everything starts becoming awkward and tiring. This is especially true for left-handers.

Cunning trick: write shorter paragraphs.

Even if you can't really improve your handwriting, this may be worth it. It's less tiring for you in the exam, because we tend to write a paragraph at a time before we stop—and this way you rest more frequently (hmm—and maybe stop to think more frequently—that could be good…). But more importantly, it's much easier for the examiner to read—he only has a short amount of information to decipher and piece together before he gets a break.

Give it three weeks at least.

You have to give it at least THREE weeks' practice. You get the new pen, you try to write big and round and slow, in shorter paragraphs, you work on the angle of your wrist, and nothing will seem to happen. Or it will seem even worse. But remember: you're trying to unlearn something you've done *millions* of times. For at least three weeks:

- Try to do *all* your work in handwriting for these three weeks
- Get a notebook; pre-date pages for three weeks; use it daily for some of your work; look at the progress from start to end. *Seeing* your progress matters
- *Consciously* practise
- Tell your teachers what you're trying to do
- Tell your parents too—you're committing yourself
- Find someone else who has problems—compete with them
- Write shorter essays—yay…
- Get a friend to check once each week and tell you what's starting to change.

After three weeks, if it's really not even starting to get a bit better, well, you've hardly lost anything. But experience suggests that it has *some* effect for about 30% of students, and a *big* effect for maybe 60% of students. *If* you try all the above, seriously.

Long-term fixes

Maybe you're reading this in the first year of the course, or maybe you're willing to do long-term work to seriously re-train your hand and brain. In that case, you need to practise. Practise. And Practise. Get hold of a serious course. Look locally, if you can.

It will very likely be worth it. For example, many employers still ask for at least some part of a job application in handwriting, and even employ professional analysts to look at them—because they are so revealing. Another reason: the 'paperless office' has been coming any time now for, what, at least thirty years. And—are you really going to write that passionate declaration of undying love in a…text?

You can easily buy pen grips from, e.g., Amazon. They helpfully point out you might choke on them. Note: the cheapest is just as likely to be just as useful as the most expensive—it depends on your fingers' shapes.

For handwriting courses, the main issue is how much they *motivate* you to keep practising, and, secondarily, how well they *diagnose* why you write awkwardly. Good teaching of handwriting is actually rather a skillful job. So, it's useful to find someone *locally*, through school / PTA / networks.

 Money Tip

Buy a few styles of pen grips, and sell those you don't like to other people in your school…

But it may work to try an online course, with regular feedback, if there's nobody near you.

A great book is *Better Handwriting*—see the *'More Reading…More'* section at the end of this book.

 Money Tip

If your handwriting really does improve, you've learnt the hard way. So, why not go down to the elementary school and offer to tutor the children with lousy handwriting? You know now what they need to do…

Deal with $peeling Porblems (Computers Ruined My Brian)

Most people have *some* spelling problems, for whatever reasons. If you think about it, it's very complex—you see black *squiggles* from which you are meant to create *sounds* in your *mind* which represent *ideas* which you turn back into *sounds* and then into abstract *squiggles* which you *write* with a pen… It actually uses many different parts of your brain working together—what's amazing is that you do this millions of times and only sometimes make mistakes.

It also means that the traditional spelling correction method—write the word out 50 times—is essentially pointless. It hasn't worked for the first 672 times you've tried to use the word, why should it work now? You need a system which gives you as many different cues to correctness as you can get, using sound, vision, imagination, and handwriting.

You also *need not to use a computer*—because in some deep part of your mind you have got into the habit of thinking 'Spellcheck', so that part of your brain is constantly saying 'I don't really need to learn this just now…I'll learn it right tomorrow…'.

Below is a *simple method* that you can use quickly, practise, and deal with maybe four words every few days. And once dealt with, they stay dealt with. This works in your situation—you have IB exams in the near future, so do you need major learning activities in addition to everything else? Fuggedaboutit.

So, you're reading this and, of course, you're saying 'Right—I'll do that list. Soon. Maybe tomorrow. Maybe…' Actually, that's a major part of your problem—dealing with spelling is something you've been putting off for years…and years…If you're going to solve the problem (and really, you know, it's not usually a huge problem) then you should just do it—today. How about making a list of 20 words ***NOW***?

It's usually comforting since it's almost certainly a shorter list than you imagined.

The simple method

Every few days, take a few words you have trouble with. You may prefer to do the following in a…private…place. Find five minutes when you probably won't be disturbed. All you need is some coloured pens, and, if you can, some Post-its of various colours, although these aren't vital. Actually, a dictionary might be useful to begin with also…

If you can create a stack of words written on Post-its then you can get friends to test you easily / quickly—frequent short tests are a very good way to improve recall.

    1. *Divide* the word into syllables—the units of sound that make up the word. So:

SYL-LA-BLE

LI-TE-RA-TURE

RHY-THM

SE-PA-RATE

    2. *Write* the word out like that on a Post-it, in CAPITAL LETTERS, each syllable in a different colour. So:

SYL-LA-BLE

LI-TE-RA-TURE

SE-PA-RATE

RHY-THM

3. *Close your eyes:*

   Say the word aloud to yourself. Separate syllable by separate syllable, as you

   Imagine it—letters and colours in your mind's eye, as you

   Write it in the air— just imagine / mime the movement of writing, as you say it aloud.

   Stick the Post-its round your house in odd memorable places...

4. *Uncover, check, repeat the whole process three times for each word.*

   That's it.

The Complex Method

This takes more time and effort, and it's only worth doing with occasional words that, for some reason, never come out ~~Write~~ right. It relies on techniques outlined in the section on how your memories work, and, particularly, the fact that your long-term memory is basically visual—you remember *faces* and *pictures* and *places* essentially perfectly. But you don't remember *words* and *ideas* perfectly—which is what most writing is about. So:

You need to turn the word into a picture in your long-term memory (that you can *consciously* consult, whenever you need to use the word)

Start by working out where you usually make the mistake in spelling. For example, I could never remember if there was an 'E' or an 'A' in the middle of *SEPARATE*.

Now create a picture which mixes the image and the sound in your mind correctly. I have to confess—my image was a deeply disliked student who was having his legs pulled ApArt by two crocodiles—they were being sepArated, and he looked like the shape of an A as his feet were spread wider...and he screamed 'AAA...'

(I know, I know, people like this shouldn't be allowed to teach).

Another example: there's one 'H' or two in '*WITHHOLD*'? Imagine the two 'H's are a couple of people desperately holding on to each other in the middle of the word.

Pigeon? does it have a 'D'? Imagine a flying PIG...

It doesn't matter how stupid the picture is; in fact, research suggests that pictures which are colourful, absurd, and rude are the best remembered.

> "So, they say hard work never hurt anybody. But I figured—why take the chance?"
>
> *Ronald Reagan, US President*

I have some bad news to start with. Probably most students revise by sitting with their huge pile of notes / hand-outs / print-outs / textbooks, re-reading them, turning the pages, nodding, saying, 'Uh huh, remember that…remember that…oops, didn't understand that…remember that…uh huh…' Students will spend hours and days re-reading their notes, sometimes highlighting them as they go. Research suggests that this is *almost completely a waste of time.* So, what should you do?

I hate to make you think at this point—you just want answers. Now. So here are Five Quick Fixes just to settle the anxiety—five things that research suggests are true for anyone revising large amounts of information. But you do have to read about the Long Careful Fixes to really be good at exams.

Revision: The Five Quick Fixes

1. Make connections about the information you're trying to learn. You can try and connect facts to each other, or attach extra information to facts you know well, or put information into a framework you already understand. But trying to remember facts without *understanding* them is very difficult and almost pointless.

2. Divide a topic into half a dozen sections and study them over different weeks. That way you get more practice thinking about the items of information. So, you take 'Cells' in Biology and study their *structure* one week, the different *kinds* of cells next week, *processes* within cells next week. Etc…

3. Repeated short tests are every effective. It looks as though it's the *effort* of trying to *retrieve* information that makes it stick in your head, not just seeing or repeating it. So, if you can find a way to give yourself tests once a week on the difficult topics, that will help. Looking at lots of past papers is effectively doing this.

4. Study early rather than late. Okay, a lot of complications here, but it's fairly clear that if you have a lot of work to do it's much better to get up early and do it, than to stay up late. If you stay up late, you think you're working, but actually you monitor yourself badly, you have micro-sleeps without knowing, your recall rate goes down, and your performance the next day usually suffers.

5. Change the *form* of the information in some way. Just looking at it, or reading it, is pointless. You can turn text into diagrams, you can make a chapter into a mind map; you could explain it to a friend or your little brother; you can make a mnemonic; you could create a test on it to give to a friend—just *do* something with it. On the next page, there are two examples of how you can do something with your written notes…

 Author's Tip

Mind maps / spider diagrams are excellent for this kind of learning.

 Author's Tips

Look at the section on Work mates—they're a very good way to do lots of short tests, and more.

Try going to bed early once in a week and once in a weekend, and getting up to work between 5–8 a.m. If nothing else, it means you've done your revision for the day and can relax in the evening.

Make cards etc. with work mates, then teach them to each other. What you *can't* teach makes a good question to ask your teacher.

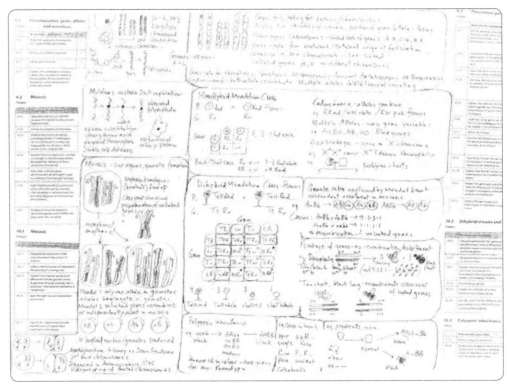

Figure 4.1: *Genetics Mind Map*

The figure above shows an example of a mind map for the genetics unit for Biology. At the sides are what the Syllabus says you should do. In the middle are diagrams and pictures (better in colour) to summarise the information.

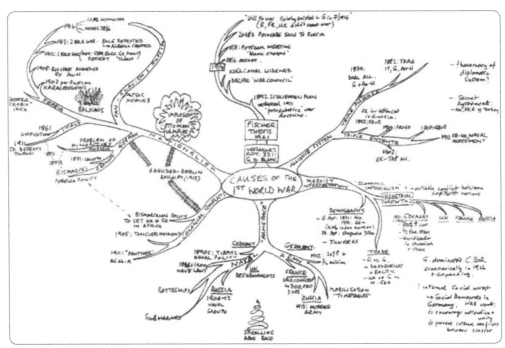

Figure 4.2: *Causes of WW1 Mind Map*

This mind map summarises the causes of WW1. It's the effort of making a map like this that's at least as useful as the final picture.

I'd like to give credit to the people who made these diagrams, but can't trace them—apologies.

Exam Preparation: The Long Careful Fixes

First, you need to understand that there are *several different kinds of testing going on in exams*, and they need different kinds of preparation.

1. Higher order skills

These are the important things being tested in IB exams. How well can you organise ideas? Can you see two sides of an argument? Could you explain why some information matters? Can you see logical sequences? Can you make logical deductions?

Higher order skills are complex and take a lot of practice in class. A book like this isn't intended to teach you to think. It can help you to fake it—look at the sections on essay writing, presentations, the Extended Essays, etc. But you actually do have to learn these skills the hard way. Sorry.

2. Factual information

In order to get tested on the higher order skills, you also need to know or remember a certain amount of information. You need to know what sequences are in the Krebs cycle, who the main leaders were during the Cold War, what the Kyoto Agreement said, etc.

And factual information you learn *individually*. Look at the section in this book on 'Memory'. There's a lot you can do in that section. Also look at the section on 'Revision', which will help you organise the learning of things.

3. Exam skills

The way those higher order skills get *tested* is by certain peculiar methods—like writing essays very fast with no references to hand, answering multiple choice questions, labelling diagrams, recording oral commentaries. These are skills you learn just so you can do exams (does any job or life experience, more than ordering a burger, involve multiple choice questions?), and you need to practise / revise them.

Exam skills you really practise mostly by *doing exams*. But below we look at some of the other ways you can improve your exam performance.

Obviously, all the above skills are connected, but you can see they are different kinds of skills. Well, maybe you can't see that, but believe me—they need different kinds of work.

How to revise *higher order* skills

1. Look at the Assessment Criteria. *Do you actually understand them?* When the Criteria for commentaries say, '…effective references to the passage…' do you know what 'effective' means? Have you seen examples? Do you know *how* to make references?

2. Use your teacher. Amazingly, they probably do want you to succeed. If you ask for five minutes of their time and have a very *specific* question about *ideas and concepts* (don't waste their time asking about facts you can just look up, or practical issues like how to show maths working); they will usually find time to help.

 Author's Tip

Try explaining the Criteria to your parents—see what you can't really explain.

 Author's Tip

Most schools have study leave just before exams, so your teachers will not have their IB class—so they'll have a little more time to help you then. Be nice. Smile.

Money Tip

If they're expensive, rent them out to other students; sell them on to IB1 when you've finished with them.

Author's Tip

Summarise in bullet points the main recommendations for a Subject Report; get friends to do the same for other subjects; swap the information.

How to revise *exam* skills

1. Past papers. Lots of them. Create a bank of them—ask your teacher, get friends whose older brother / sister may have them. Go online and buy them from the IBO. You can't have too many. *Make sure they're the right syllabus* (they change every seven or eight years…)!

2. *Lots* of *quick* practices with past papers. If you're doing multiple choice, don't actually write anything—do them with a friend who has the answers and just say your answer. If you're doing essay questions, just bullet point the three main points you'd make, in ten minutes. If you're doing a commentary, just note the five main areas you'd discuss. For Maths, just be confident you could show the working. Etc.

3. Get hold of the Subject (Examiners') Reports from previous years. Ask your teacher or the IBDPC for them, politely…These are long, seriously boring, but gold-dust! They will tell you section by section, paper by paper, what students typically do well or badly in the exams.

How to revise *factual information*

This is what worries most people—it's actually the easiest one to organise and get right.

1. Look at the section later in this book on how your memories work. That gives you half a dozen things you can do.

2. Make note cards (Remember? Colours, rude images, not much writing…). If you do this with a friend you can get double the quantity of information sorted.

3. Test yourself and your friends regularly—once a week, very quick short tests on part of a topic. If you get it right, hooray. If a lot is wrong, go back and re-write the cards etc., and test again.

Ten great ways to revise with work mates

- Make note cards to share.

- Explain concepts to each other.

- Summarise Subject (Examiners') Reports for each other.

- Get past papers to look at together.

- Identify problems you both / all have, to ask teachers about.

- Write summary posters of units / topics on a big piece of paper.

- Test each other on the definitions in science syllabuses.

- Write Post-its to put round your houses.

- Learn two quotations per exam text per session you meet—then test each other next time.

- Test each other on understanding the Assessment Criteria .

Revision in 120 Hours

It's very odd really. Most IB students seem to believe that if they don't think about them, the final exams will just take care of themselves. They live in denial—don't prepare; don't get organized. And then suddenly it gets to the point where they really can't be ignored and its all pain and panic and sweating and bewilderment. They really wish they'd listened to what they'd been told about how to prepare… but it's all too late.

And here's the thing: as distant and terrifying as they may seem, you really can make the experience of exams an awful lot easier and pleasanter if you do some preparation.

Make a list of topics

Get your textbook or your notes or your syllabus outline or a revision guide for each subject.

Make a very rough list of topics you need to revise (Note: you won't need to revise everything you've studied). Just a word or two to describe, and remember: a topic is enough, e.g., Development Economics, International Economics, Macroeconomic Models…

Just believe this: 80 x 80

A useful rule of thumb is: plan for 80 revision sessions of 80 minutes.

The reasoning for this, if you care…For each course, vast OSC experience suggests a rule of thumb: you need to spend about 10% of the time you spent studying on revision. Total: about 120 hours. Another rule of thumb: you can do a useful work session of 80 minutes if you take some breaks. So…

80 sessions of 80 minutes: 16–18 sessions each HL, 9–10 for each SL.

Allocate sessions to topics

Okay, so now you can see what needs doing. 80 sessions in which you can revise; just start allocating them from that list. You probably know what subjects you need to spend more or less time on. So, you end up saying something like:

'I've got sixteen sessions available for Physics HL; I've got this list I made of 12 topics to revise; I've given them priorities, so now I know I've got two hours for electro-magnetism, two hours for gravitation, etc…' And if you look at that and say 'OMG—how am I going to revise gravitation in two hours?', well, that's actually extremely helpful. You start thinking about whether your priorities need changing, whether you'll work some Saturdays, how to make your revision more efficient…

 Author's Tip

It won't just be revision… At the end of January, ask your teacher what the priorities are, *and* what new topics you have left to study (and of course, later revise…).

 Author's Tip

You're never going to follow a schedule exactly, but thinking about each session helps you allocate your time, and you'll make better use of 80 minutes if you have a target.

 Author's Tip

Get your exam schedule from your IBDPC (or download it—you can get a personalised copy from osc-ib.com, or a general version direct from ibo.org). Allocate revision in the order of your exams—you'll have a little time between later exams to carry on revising.

How Do I Get Inside an Examiner's Head?

Five things that make examiners hate you

It's a really interesting exercise to get students to guess beforehand what these hateful things might be…But no time for that.

Anyway, it's all about the money. You need to understand this: IB examiners usually get paid for each individual paper, or essay, or section, or test, or whatever that they mark. So, if they get paid $10 for an essay and they can mark five in an hour, they get $50 an hour—they're in a good mood. If they can only mark 2 in an hour, they're losing money—they're in a foul mood. You cost them money: they hate you.

Do *you* want to be one of the students that make the examiner *lose money* as they decide how to grade your paper?

A. Yes?

B. No?

Well, here are some of the ways that you lose the examiner money:

1. **Lousy handwriting.** Big problem. You spend all these years being told to type / print everything you give in, then suddenly have to handwrite for hours. You do it badly, messily. The examiner tries to follow, but they're *losing money* all the time they spend trying to decipher *your* handwriting…You can do a lot for your handwriting in less than a month. Do it.

2. **Cut and Paste.** Similar to the above—a computer habit. It emerges more and more often now in exams—students adding notes in the margin; putting brackets round paragraphs and arrows to show they should be read elsewhere; extra 'bonus' paragraphs at the end of essays; massive footnotes; asterisked notes; huge crossing out of sections. Sound familiar? Takes a long time to read, so…

3. **Vomit essays.** Where students who know a lot of information just throw it *all* up onto the page and pray the examiner will sort it out (clear up the mess…). *Your job is to use information to answer a question, not to prove how much you know.* Examiners won't waste time (and their money, remember?) organising your ideas for you.

4. **What's s/he writing about?** Small irritation, but a bad way for you to start. You should indicate which question or topic or passage you're writing about. In Language essays, it's good to indicate in the first paragraph which texts you're going to write about as well. That way the examiner isn't wasting precious limited energy trying to work out if you're answering the right question or just rambling inexplicably.

5. **Wrong section.** Heartbreakingly common—especially in Language A where students have studied say, poetry for the final exam, but then decide, bizarrely, or by ignorance, to answer a question on drama. The examiners loses time checking—and you lose 20% of your marks automatically.

Author's Tip

Read the section on Handwriting in this book. Try reading old handwritten essays by other students. Yech.

Author's Tip

Always, always, always plan the three main points of what you're going to say *before you start writing. Always*. Got that? Then you won't be changing it as you go along.

Author's Tip

Always, always, always plan the three main points of what you're going to say *before you start writing. Always.* (Oh—did I say that already? Must be important then).

Author's Tip

Writing out the question is a waste of time—just write the number.

Author's Tip

Look at last year's paper and *check with your teacher* before the exam. In class. In public. *Don't* be embarrassed about sounding stupid. In any group of ten students, I guarantee *four* will be secretly astonished and / or grateful—and one will still get it wrong.

Can I think like an examiner?

Sun Tzu in *The Art of War* says you can only win if you can think like your opponent. Even better, if you could swap places with your opponent in your mind. So, it is with IB exams and examiners—you'll get better grades if you spend a little time thinking about what 'They' want from you…So remember:

- *Examiners are not hairy red-eyed monsters from Mars*, nor a weird species of vat-grown academics—they're almost all just ordinary teachers (like yours, maybe) who need the money.

- *There are no secrets.* The IBO really wants to be transparent—you should know everything you want to know about the examining process, and how your work gets graded. Examiners do not get some secret training or instructions that you aren't ever going to know about.

- *Students can mark almost as accurately as examiners*, if they want to—they just need the Assessment Criteria and very little practice.

So, if you do some of the following things, you can rather quickly start thinking like an examiner, understand what they want to see and read—and give it to them…

Practise grading papers

Just get an essay, or whatever, from another student, and try to grade it using the Assessment Criteria. The more often you do this, the better you get at it. You start seeing how important particular words in the Criteria are in choosing which grade to give.

Get the Subject Reports

Seriously boring, but fantastically valuable (oh—how many times have I said that?). After every exam session the examiners write a report giving masses of advice on exactly what candidates are doing well or badly in each part of exams, and how to do better. Get last year's reports from your teachers (nag them every day—you are meant to have access to them).

Write your own practice questions

It's a great way to start understanding how carefully IB questions are put together and how carefully you need to read them. The big trick is: can you see what kind of answer you are trying to get from the candidate? Can you outline the main points of reasonable answers to the question you wrote? At least do a few multiple-choice questions.

Get past papers and questions

Get them from teachers, older brothers. And if desperate—buy them from the IBO itself. Look at their website ibo.org.

 Author's Tip

Copy a piece of student work, like your last piece of homework for example, and grade it using the Criteria, with four other students. Compare grades at break time one day. If the five grades are similar, you're learning well. If they're very *different*, you've learnt a really important lesson—*you don't know why work is graded as good or bad,* so in the final exam, how can you do what the examiner wants to see?

 Author's Tip

Get a group of you and each get the Subject Report for a different subject. Bullet point the main recommendations (usually near the end of the report) and copy and distribute them to the others.

 Money Tip

Sell the bullet-pointed recommendations to the class—wouldn't you pay for 'The ten best bits of advice on how to do the exam', from the people who *set* the exam?

 Money Tip

Start a fund and try to write questions you think will come up in the actual exam. Anyone who correctly predicts a question, gets the fund…

Things that make examiners laugh, or cry

"I never did well on exams, except for the coal mining exams. They're not difficult, they just ask you 'What's your name?' and I got seventy-five per cent on that one."

Peter Cook

The exams, and their procedures, are surprisingly complex, or at least they seem to take about 8,000 IB students a year by surprise—that's about how many students seem to lose marks in the final exams by doing something, that's, well…dumb.

Classic exam mistakes

- Didn't turn to the back page of the question booklet
- Turned over two pages together of the question booklet
- Answered the wrong section—especially in Language A
- Wrote too many essays
- Wrote too few essays
- Spelt the names of characters / texts / writers / elements / major figures incorrectly
- Didn't show the working in Maths
- Didn't show how they used the calculator
- Didn't show limits of error in measurements
- Forgot to write their candidate number
- Crossed out their answer instead of their notes / working
- Crossed out the working but then didn't replace it with new working.

Oh, and much more, and worse. Of course, you would never do something like that—but that's what they thought also, no?

> **So—just do these:**
> - Lots of practice with past papers
> - Check a paper in class with your teacher
> - Make sure you have seen an exam paper in the current format (formats change regularly)
> - Use the reading time .

Exam Day—Too Late?

You know that idiot question people ask you when you're about to go out the door on a trip: 'Have you got everything?' Well, are you ever going to say 'No' as the result of being asked?

I mean, okay, have spare pens, check your calculator batteries, check traffic reports and have a taxi number for emergencies, wear clean underwear (statistically, some candidate somewhere will go to hospital instead of the exam…) etc., but you know all this, and what's the point of saying it to you if you don't know or believe? You must have a brain the size of a pigeon's if you don't take a spare pen. Oh, all right:

- *Two* spare pens, black
- Pencils and eraser
- Coloured pens if needed
- Highlighters
- Watch
- Calculator
- Calculator batteries?
- Tissues
- Glasses
- Water
- Medication—especially for hayfever (in May…) and asthma.

Just before the exam

- Read your notecards if it makes you feel less nervous.
- Do your breathing exercises (see section 'Panic: square breathing, the quick fix').

In the exam

- *Read carefully.* This is why the IB gives you time to read the paper before the exam starts.
- *Read Carefully. The questions cost a lot of money.* They're proposed, discarded, argued about, tested, discussed in expensive committees, tried out in schools, etc. etc. etc. *Every word* matters.
- *Check your work.* Research and experience suggest that students can e.g. self-correct 80% of language mistakes if they stop to look. And that's in ordinary home-work….It's even more true of work done under exam pressure.
- *Plan.* You really absolutely must know what you are going to say before you start writing. Look at the section on what examiners hate…
- *Just enough fear.* Of course, you'll be nervous, and some adrenaline will helpfully speed up your thinking and release energy. Too much will make you panic…
- *Answer the question. Don't* try to prove how much you know—that's *not* what it's about.

 Author's Tip

Look at last year's paper before you go to the exam, and list the three main instructions. Check these against *this* year's instructions when you read—that way you're thinking about them instead of just skipping through.

 Author's Tip

No question is casual or approximate in any way. So, read *every* word of the question. It means something *exact.*

 Author's Tip

Always leave four minutes at the end to check at least the first paragraph of anything you write.

 Author's Tip

Three good points for an essay is a good rule of thumb—and mention what they are in the first paragraph.

Author's Tip

Read the section in this book on panic and practise for the two weeks before the exams. Get conscious control of how nervous you are.

Author's Tip

If you cheated, lied, or plagiarised in some way that means that it may be that you are hoping to fool your teacher, then an examiner, and then maybe two, even three other examiners. Oh well—try it if you want. But...

It ain't over till it's over

It's just, *just,* worth understanding this, because it tells you two important things.

1. Your work gets sent away to an examiner who grades it, and whose grading is checked against standards and by senior examiners who are very close to God.

2. Your final grade is then checked by a computer against your *predicted grade*. If it varies by more than two grades either way then it gets re-marked. It's a fairly robust, accurate system.

It's good but not perfect. Nobody wants to admit it but every year there are new examiners who just don't get it, administrative mess ups, questions that didn't quite work. But it's usually accurate. If you want to appeal against a grade, *ask your teacher first* what they think—not your parents, your friend, probably not even your IBDPC. And remember: grades can go *up* or *down* on appeal.

> 'You've got the brain of a four-year old child, and I bet they were glad to get rid of it...'
>
> *Marx (Groucho...)*

"Life is like a sewer—you only get out of it what you put into it..."

Tom Lehrer

Definite Big Problems

Okay, it does happen that there will always be students who have a *real* problem with something—access to working spaces, handwriting that's just unavoidably bad, major spelling issues, can't concentrate for the whole length of an exam paper, whatever. And these are often pretty much beyond the control of the student.

The IBO recognises that this is the case, and it can and will make allowances, like being able to use a laptop to write, extra time in exams, added breaks, and so forth. If you need these forms of assistance, you can get them.

But, you need to prove you need the help, and prove that fact pretty much at the start of the course. And it can take a few months before that to get testing done and certified.

So, if you or your parents or your teachers think you may need 'Accommodation' as it's called, you'll need to start doing something about it as soon on in the course *as you possibly can.* If in any doubt, just go and talk to the IBDPC right at the start of the course if possible.

Memory—How To

(And why taking notes isn't what you thought…)

The IB is like most exam systems: one thing you have to be able to do is remember rather a lot of information about quite a lot of topics for a few months very well. Then you need to access it very quickly for a very short time. Then you need to forget it.

Actually, the IB is better than many systems—most of the memorising effort is actually tested by how well you understand and can use the information. But still, you're not likely to be chatting at parties about, say, Oxidative Photophosphorylation, in later life. So, what you basically need is ways to remember a lot, quickly, for a relatively short time.

Here are some practical tricks. But if you're going to believe they'll work, you need to understand just a little bit of theory. And maybe you'll want convincing that they work or are worth the effort—so try the experiment at the end.

Psychology students—I know the following description isn't exactly right, but it's good enough to get the idea, no?

Essentially, a good way to think of it is that you have *several different kinds of memory.*

Particularly, you have a:

- **Buffer Memory:** this is really just recycling information in a kind of holding area between your ears for periods of seconds, less than minutes. It's quite small—usually you can reckon on about seven items of information. It's what you use to remember, e.g., telephone numbers (you know how you repeat them to yourself to keep them in your memory…) or it's how you can answer your teachers when they bark at you. So what did I just say? Hey?

  Things have to go through your Buffer Memory on their way to the next memory. *They will only go through if you have understood them in some way.* Random strings of numbers, background music, theories you didn't quite grasp, books you skip-read without understanding, droning classroom lectures—all that is just short-circuited here.

  If you want to get things through this Buffer Memory and remember them, you have to process or encode the things you heard—you have to *change the form of the information* from sounds / words into notes, or pictures, or diagrams, or a story, or whatever. But you must do *something*—that's why you take notes.

- **Day-Long Memory:** *If* you processed the information, understood it in some way, then this is where you'll hold information for about 24 hours. It's usually in the form of *ideas*, of *meaning*. If you try really hard, you can probably recall a lot of what you were told today (if you understood it), in every lesson. But you'd find it hard. That's another reason why you took notes. Some of it is starting to fade already, especially what's not been properly encoded—the stuff you didn't really understand very well.

  There's good reason why this memory lasts about 24 hours. It's because you're going to go to sleep. That's when most of it will be transferred to the next memory. That's largely what sleep is for to give your brain time to sort out this information and store it. If you don't sleep enough, the brain starts losing information…

- **Long-Term Memory (LTM):** a huge amount of information can, and usually is, stored here. No, you can't memorise the Encyclopaedia Britannica; no, your brain doesn't have more connections than the universe (long-lasting urban legends). But it's huge—a lot more than you need to remember *everything* from a year or two of IB classes (even *decades* of IB classes—now there's a thought to chill the blood…).

Two main things to know about LTM, that will help you remember that exciting stuff about Born-Haber cycles and Eukaryotic DNA:

1. *LTM information is stored in a network of connections*, and you can learn to create and control these networks—but it takes some conscious organised effort. You'll probably only want to do that when it's really needed.

2. *LTM loves images, pictures, visuals.* You'll remember people's faces for years, not their names. You remember that colourful diagram on the bottom left page of your textbook, not what all that writing said. This is something you can make good use of, quite easily.

How to make your memories work better

Lots of short sessions

You remember much better the *beginnings* and *ends* of things—like lists, lessons, chapters, lectures, relationships, revision sessions…Study and revise and work in lots of short sessions, so you have lots of beginnings and endings.

Frequent short reviews

If you learn, then revise something, then just leave it; it fades—you know that. Find a way to *quickly* review what you've studied every couple of weeks.

Lots of short tests

It's the *effort* of trying to recall information that strengthens the connections in the LTM networks, and makes information more easily accessible.

Use colours and images and spaces between information

Use lots of highlighters, diagrams, and coloured cards.

Get enough sleep

Seriously. Read the section about how to get to sleep, and why your brain will rot if you don't.

How to make your memories amazingly good

Remember that long-term memory works very effectively with images. Here are three ways to make use of that.

1. *Note cards.* Take topics, and reduce the main points to just seven images / diagrams / pictures / shapes / phrases. The images can be as complex as you like. Try not to make them too small. Draw these on to large coloured note cards (you can get them in most big stationery shops). If you must use words, write them in capital letters.

   These are brilliant in several ways: the effort of making them makes strong LTM connections; it forces understanding or questions; they are very easy to recall; they're very good for quick reviews; and, they're great for testing other people.

2. *Quick image lists (up to ten items).* Make a single mental image with all the items in the same image, as symbols, objects, and words. Use people or objects as 'hooks' to hang the items on, such as a rubbish tip, the door of a club, a teacher you hate, a statue, your dog. Don't use things that close / hide (like a bag, a book, a drawer…). See the example on the next page in the box.

 Author's Tips

Try several *20-minute* study sessions (when did you really ever concentrate all through a 40-minute lesson?)

Work with friends—meet once a week for five minute mini-tests to test each other on different topics. Repeat the tests once in a while.

Try turning pages of notes into mind maps; use lots of coloured pens, pictures, and no more than seven words. Very hard the first time; it gets much easier.

 Author's Tip

Try doing a few of these note cards after sections of your work even in the first year—they'll save huge amounts of revision time in the second year.

 Author's Tip

Make sure you imagine it all in technicolour and preferably make the images rude (research shows adolescents are *amazingly* good at recalling rude pictures…).

3. *Memory mansions.* More complex, harder work, big results…Make a pile of all the information you need to remember on a topic. Now imagine a friend's apartment or house, and start putting the information into the house in the form of imagined portraits, graffiti, statues, posters, people, animals…Imagine yourself walking around it, looking at all these things you've put in there. Make it as bizarre as you like—what goes on in your head, stays in your head.

Image memories

For example, six things you need to remember about Chinese politics in the 1920's (okay, this may seem random, but it's actually taken from an IB History revision guide which gives six points you need to remember…).

In the hallway there's a statue of Chiang Kai-shek, subduing warlords, a *model train* on the floor, a *picture* of primary schools growing, someone's spray painted *graffiti* saying 'Academica Sinica', a *parrot's* squawking 'diplomats, eh?', your friend's *mother* puts money in your pocket and whispers to you 'He reformed finances, dear.'

You won't forget that picture easily, if you've put even minimal effort into really seeing it in your mind.

Quotations (and remember that's really the correct word, not 'quotes'…)

These seem to worry a lot of students. How many to remember? Long or short? More for poetry or not? etc.

Actually, you can perfectly well get an excellent grade just by making close reference to the texts, but if you want to learn quotations, here's a good way:

1. Choose quotations which illustrate relevant aspects of theme, setting, character development, conflicts, etc., and which also illustrate characteristic features of the author's style of writing.

2. Write them individually on notecards, preferably a different colour for each text. Get a friend (or friends) to do the same. Make a stack of cards and keep them in your pocket.

3. Whenever you see your friends, take out a card and give them the first half of a quotation and they should finish it. Next time give them fewer and fewer words as cues. Give a prize for the one who ends up able to get all the quotations correct given just the first word.

Experiment

So many clever ideas in the world—are they worth the effort? Try this. Don't cheat. It takes five minutes. If it works, then maybe I'm telling you the truth about other things…

Part 1. Just read twice this list of items from a shopping list:

'Tomatoes, coffee, bacon, pharmacy, post a letter, batteries, pen, newspaper, juice.'

Now read the section on 'How to make money in the IB' for *five minutes*.

Now try to write the list. I guess you're going to try and cheat because your schooling has conditioned you to try and really impress people. How awful is that?

Part 2. Now try this list, but with method number 2.

I'll talk you through it; really try to draw the picture in your mind.

'Potatoes, eggs, carrots, mend the bike, pen, stamps, balloons, dog food, visit the doctor, pins.'

Lady riding a *bike*; she's *throwing up*; *balloons* tied to her thumbs; she looks a bit startled because she's sitting on a *pin*. One earring's a *carrot*; the other is a *potato*. She's got a broken *egg* smashed on her head; it's dripping down to a *stamp* stuck on her nose, and a *pen* up one nostril. She's got a dog in a basket swinging from the handlebars.

See how many of the items you can remember after five minutes.

Two ways your memory *doesn't* work

70% or more of students revise by opening that big folder of notes / hand-outs / print-outs / papers—and re-reading them. All you're doing there is recognising information, not recalling it. It has no measurable effect on your memory. Go for a walk instead. Or go to sleep.

Working really, really hard the night before the exam. Actually, your brain just doesn't have enough time (you need several hours awake) to process the information you learn very late at night. All you're doing is getting tired for the next day.

Panic, Nerves, Fear

Anyone who feels no nervousness at the thought of standing in front of a large audience is probably missing part of their brain. Almost literally. Evolution spent *millions* of years training our ancestors to realise when they were being watched by potentially hostile audiences and instinctively react—the ones who didn't learn that got eaten. So, you *should* feel a bit nervous and that comes from quite deep down in the reptile brain. It's no use just trying to say to yourself it's all going to be fine. You actually have to control your lizard brain…

What that deep part of your brain is doing is preparing you for the sensible response to threats: to fight or to run away. If you had to *think* about that, it would take too long, so it all gets done unconsciously—the brain starts pumping up the adrenalin to get the muscles and reflexes ready, and you're not even aware of it. You just get the symptoms—a bit shaky, faster breathing, butterflies in the stomach, wobbly knees, mind goes a bit blank…

(It's usually at this point some well-meaning idiot teacher coos 'Hey, it's going to be *fine*…' or even barks 'LISTEN! Just **RELAX!** And you want, instinctively, to thwack them upside the head.)

Quite rightly, because what you have here is a *physical* problem with adrenalin and muscles—and words and good thoughts are pretty much pointless. You need a *physical* response. You could use chemicals to control your responses but these may not be recommendable when you need a clear head…Try this:

Panic: square breathing, the quick fix

You need to control your breathing above all, and, luckily, this is quite easy to do and not very public. It also has the advantage that you won't forget how to do it. The method is called 'square breathing', and versions of it are used by cynical professional actors of all kinds, so it must work.

- *Breathe in slowly,* deeply, during the count of *four* (1…2…3…4)
- *Hold* it for the count of *four*
- *Breathe right out,* empty your lungs, during the count of *four*
- *Hold it* for the count of *four*
- Then do the whole round for the count of *five*
- Then for the count of *six*
- Then the count of *five*
- Then the count of *four…*

It takes about three minutes; you can repeat it; once you get the hang of it then it starts to work more quickly because you create a learned reflex of relaxation. You need to *think* about it and count the numbers to yourself. It's *amazing* how well this works. See tutorials on YouTube.

Panic: the big slow fix

The quick fix works for just about every situation that the typical IB student is ever likely to face: commentaries, presentations, school assemblies, asking for the first date, lying to your teacher in public, telling your parents what happened at that party…

But if you get really *seriously* nervous (and you're not going the pharmaceutical control route…) then you're going to have to learn serious relaxation for your muscles. You have to break the feedback whereby your brain tells your muscles to tense up, so they get tense, so the reptile part of your brain thinks there must be a threat, so it sends out more adrenalin to prepare to fight or fly, so your muscle gets more tense so…Etc. You have to educate your muscles, teach them new reflexes, and, like learning anything to do with the body (think of learning to throw with your other hand, any new sport, juggling…), this takes time and practice.

A very good system is called 'progressive muscle relaxation'—I describe it in in the section on 'Insomnia', and you can also find some good video clips showing it on YouTube.

It may be that you get *really seriously nervous*, in which case you have to learn serious control. You can try systems like tai chi, or yoga or meditation, or psychological methods like cognitive behavioural therapy, which will need professional help. All these rely on developing new habits in thinking or in the body, and that takes time, but it can be done.

But the IB is really not that important, honestly—just practise working on the Square Breathing.

So—some nervousness is *normal* and *necessary*. And if you think there's too much, there are ways to deal with it. Either way, you don't need to make yourself more worried and get caught up in a vicious spiral.

Can't Sleep

It's not too surprising if you start getting to the point where you don't sleep too well, especially in the weeks before or during exams. Almost certainly it's psychological stress, emerging as a physical problem of being unable to sleep, and almost certainly it's going to be completely pointless telling yourself to relax. You get stuck in a vicious cycle of feedback whereby you're lying awake and you start to worry about not sleeping so that makes you more worried, so it's harder to sleep so you worry more about not sleeping—so you etc.…

Actually, there is, extraordinarily, a magic fairy that can help this time. 90% of insomnia can be stopped by teaching your muscles to relax. It's really that simple.

The method described below is very easy—try it as you lie in bed and can't sleep.

Here comes the sleep fairy

The best way to do this is to have a friend read the instructions aloud to you as you're lying down. Or record them yourself—read very slowly indeed—and play it back to yourself.

- Lie on the bed, head on a good pillow.
- Close your eyes and breathe very deeply two or three times—breathe right in, and then empty your lungs completely.
- What you're going to do is tighten up the muscles of different parts of your body in turn; keep them tight while you count silently to five; then let go and imagine the tension going out as you relax and smooth the muscles. *As you feel your muscles relax and get longer, you keep the sensation going as long as you can.*
- Start with your hands. Make a fist as tight as you can, hold them for five seconds, and then let your fingers open and feel the muscles relax and get longer—let the feeling continue.
- Now your face. Squint your eyes, tighten your teeth and jaw, and wrinkle your forehead. Imagine someone is going to punch you in the face. Feel the tension while you count silently to five, and then let go of it. Feel the warmth of relaxation coming to your face.
- Next, pull your shoulders up until they nearly touch your ears. Feel the tension while you count silently to five. Then let your shoulders drop.
- Now progress through the rest of your body, tightening muscles while you count slowly to five, then letting the tension go. Start with your stomach and chest muscles—think that someone is going to jump on you—then your lower abdomen, buttocks, and thighs.
- Finish with your lower legs, curling up your toes and tightening calf muscles to feel the tension in your foot, ankle, calves, and knee—imagine someone is threatening to stick a needle deep in the muscles—then relax them.
- When you have finished, notice the tension and release in all your muscles. Breathe out deeply a few times, and feel relaxed…

If you do it right, you'd find it almost impossible to repeat the process immediately. Try it, and see.

> **The Big Sleep Fairy**
>
> Any one of the above things can work. But a *combination* of *exercise,* a warm *bath*, drinking *chamomile tea*, and then doing the *muscle relaxation*…Goodnight…

Last Trick

If all else fails, get up and actually *do* some of the work that's stuck in your mind. I usually find that the mere *thought* of getting up and doing some writing on this book sends me to sleep immediately.

Author's Tip

Obviously you're more likely to sleep if your muscles are needing sleep to recover—so get some exercise each day, even if it's just a walk around the school campus a few times.

Author's Tip

Those herbal remedies that granny loves? Actually, teas made from chamomile or valerian do have an effect. Have a cup before bed.

Author's Tip

Cooling down a little is one of the cues that tells your body it's time to sleep. Have a warm bath or shower about half an hour before you go to bed, and as you cool down your body is getting sleep signals.

My Teacher Hates Me / I Hate My Teacher

Well, of course the basic advice about hateful teachers is usually that life is like that, get over it…so that really helps, doesn't it? More usefully, you first need to consider these two rather different scenarios:

1. *Your teacher is a **bad** teacher.* Are they late, disorganised, badly informed, can't explain concepts, don't finish topics? These are professional issues, and if you and other students see them, then the chances are that the school does also and is working on it—but would never tell you about it.

2. *You **dislike** your teacher.* There's a personality clash; you have very different styles; you get into public arguments? It's sensible to consider here what they would say about you and be horribly honest.

Remember: these issues are different—you can have a lazy slob of a teacher who you actually like a lot and a frightening rude teacher who really gets you to work well.

What to do?

- *Accept nothing much is going to change*—schools aren't geared to changing things because of students really, and teachers mostly don't think they're doing something wrong.

- *Don't argue more than once.* And save that for when it really matters—and mostly it doesn't matter. But what actually do you think is the purpose—what will you be able to change as a result of this argument? The most it will possibly do is make you feel better. And the situation worse.

- *Don't fall into generalising*—so they shouted at you once, unreasonably? Don't start seeing that happening all the time.

- *Break it down into specific issues*—so they're sarcastic to you in class, but do they mark you unfairly, or shout, or forget to do things, or give you undeserved lousy reports?

- *Negotiate about the specific issues,* and only about those. See the section on 'Manage Your Teacher'.

- *Get a sensible friend to watch what happens in class*, and tell you a truthful opinion. Don't just get the kind of person who tells you what you want to hear.

- *Work out what exactly triggers the behaviour* that you don't like—can you avoid triggering it? Staying silent and thinking about more important things can avoid 80% of triggers.

- *Absolute nuclear melt-down case*—spend a month documenting every interaction you have with that teacher, and then go talk to a school counsellor, or another teacher you can trust (but remember: it's probably more important to them to have a good colleague for ten years than an unhappy student for a few months…). And be prepared for a lousy time—is it really worth it? Maybe it is.

Procrastination and Your Reptile Brain

'The only thing I finish is dessert…'

Do you recognise any of these?

- You often, or usually, leave your coursework to the last evening before it's due.
- You often find yourself doing lots of small unnecessary jobs when there's a big job to do.
- You have a pile-up of jobs to do that you really are ignoring, and you know it.
- You quite often end up working really late, caffeine-fuelled, frenzied, irritated, swearing you'll never do this again…

Okay, this is normal. It's built into being human. There isn't a language in the world without a word for 'putting things off'. Aristotle wrote about it ('malakia'); the ancient Egyptians had eight hieroglyphics for it; the Hawaiians call it 'napa'—what do you call it? There have been literally thousands of academic studies of it, all with the same conclusions. It occurs in all cultures. Adults learn ways to deal with it; adolescents find it harder. Men procrastinate more than women, in any culture. Students have the worst problems.

Does it matter? It may do—only you know. Below are 16 ways to deal with minor timewasting (70%+ of people do this) and chronic delaying that damages (20% of people have major problems).

Your parent(s) may have to be your pre-frontal cortex

But first you need just a little theory to understand the suggested solutions to the problem. Basically, it looks as though one of the older and more animal-like (specifically, more *reptile*) parts of your brain, the limbic system, is very influential—it's the part that gives you the urges for immediate pleasure. It's what makes you want to have lots of salty fatty fast foods, quick laughs, another drink, instant fun on a video game, fast cars—oh, you know.

It's what babies have—when they want something, they want it *now,* and it's usually a pleasure they want. But as the brain starts to grow, a new area starts to build up, called the pre-frontal cortex. This is the part of the brain that seems to be about willpower, about learning and being able to make choices. Gradually you learn to hold off, to share toys, to not unwrap your present before lunch. You start to say 'I want a huge greasy cheeseburger now, but maybe I'll wait till I get a proper supper at home.'

But here's the kicker. Your pre-frontal cortex typically keeps developing until the whole brain is finished. Around about 20+ years old. Oops. So, until then, for lots of you, your parents have to act as your pre-frontal cortex—stopping you having what you want now, making you eat a proper supper instead of junk food, making you go to sleep occasionally, saying 'No fast cars', and…heck…all the fun things.

Worse: as an IB student, there's so little good for the limbic system going on. It's all about learning to organise, control, delay, plan—and all the rewards are weeks, months, even years away. There's just not a lot of pleasure involved in writing an essay due in three weeks' time, no instant fun in writing an Internal Assessment for next month. And you don't have much pressure from the pre-frontal cortex—often, you don't need to do the work just *now*—so your limbic system kicks in, and there you are on Facebook just for ten minutes, really, just ten minutes of pleasure, instantly.

The more instantly you can get pleasure, the more likely it is you'll go for it.

So, start by working out what generally (or specifically) prevents you from getting the jobs done. You can be brutally honest here—nobody's going to know or judge. And then you look at the list below of 16 ways to get over the problem: you choose what seems to apply; maybe you give yourself 15 minutes a day to work on the problem with one of the solutions. 15 minutes? Anyone can do 15 minutes. Don't do more.

Think—which one, or combination, of these, is preventing you from getting started?

- It's a horrible job.
- You're afraid of failing.
- There are so much more enjoyable things to do.
- You want it to be perfect.
- It *can* be put off.
- You just don't want to spend hours of your life on it.
- You suspect you can't do it.
- You're sulking.
- You can't bring yourself to care.

16 possible ways to deal with procrastination

Just get started

Break up The Job. It's much easier to get started on a small job than a big one—so break that big job like the writing the Extended Essay draft into lots of small jobs (write the opening sentence only; bullet point the three main points; write the first point in the body…) and do them one by one.

Do something, anything. Just write the first sentence, *only* that. Or the last sentence. Or the title. Or bullet point the three main ideas. You've started.

Buy a timer. Set it for 15 minutes. Do as much as you can until the timer sounds, then—and here's the really important thing—walk away. Finish. Don't feel bad; don't think of the rest to do; don't worry about it—just do something else. You can go back to it some other time.

See the issue

Get a calendar. Cross off all the days you can't or won't work—trips, holidays, visits, Friday evenings, Saturday nights, competitions, matches, performances…Be absolutely ruthless / realistic. You start seeing when you *have* to work.

The Big List. Produce a List of *all* the jobs you need to do. Colour code just the ones which are both important and urgent. See if you can do just those.

The Big List 2. On that Big List, colour code the jobs you just know you're not doing because you don't *want* to do them. It's awful to think of doing *all* of them. Try doing just *one* unpleasant job a day until they've gone away.

Target. Don't say in the evening, 'I'll do my homework…'. List exactly what you need to do, as specifically as possible: 'Three maths problems, write the plan for the history essay, and write up one lab.' As you finish each one, give yourself a few minutes of something fun. If you get stuck on one of them, don't fight it, move on to another task, get it done, have some fun…

Use people

Work with a friend. Set a joint deadline when you have to meet after school and show the work to each other. In drastic cases, put 50 rupees into a pot—if either of you don't have the work, the other person gets the money.

Confess. Talk to your teacher—before the last minute. Tell them it's a real problem. See if they can understand, or even help…

Contracts with your parents. Arrange some system with them that will just be embarrassing for you if you don't live up to it: 'If I don't meet 80% of my deadlines this month, you can choose which two nights I can't go out…' 'I'll write all my deadlines on a calendar in the kitchen and cook every day that I miss a deadline, until it's done…'

Routines

Get some routines. It takes energy to decide to do something, and makes it harder to start. Make a decision *once* that, e.g., you'll always work from say 7 to 9 on four evenings a week, and Tuesdays and Thursdays after school in a classroom. Just keep that routine. You're not having to fight that decision every day and so every day giving yourself chance to think of good reasons to work…tomorrow…

Morning routines. Once a fortnight, on the same morning each time, get up early and do two hours of work before school. Fewer distractions, a clear end to the work each time, it's all bonus achievement…you may be surprised how much you can get done.

Live with it

Plan when to be distracted. You may know that you just *have* to spend two hours a day on Facebook or you'll be a social outcast. So—*schedule* that, maybe in two routine evening blocks. Makes it harder to persuade yourself you'll just check for five minutes, really, just five…

*Sometimes you **do** get work done.* So work out what makes it happen then—is it because the job is *easy,* or *quick*, or you don't *care*, or you can do it *90% okay*, or you have more *energy* sometimes, or you worked with a *friend*, or got *started at school*…And then start re-creating those conditions occasionally.

Take consolation: you may put things off, but probably not as badly as Victor Hugo. He found it so hard to get on with writing his books that he would give his clothes to his servant at the beginning of the day, and was only given them back if he could prove he'd written something.

Facebook Made Me Fail the IB

You know as well as I do that, if you're working at home, maybe 20% of your time is spent just really, really, quickly checking Facebook, or that game-site, or seeing that great YouTube clip, or whatever…really, just really, quickly…Oh and I'll just text…She said whaaaat?…But just ten minutes checking about that guy in…Etc.

And after that 20% of your time disappears, you spend another 10% trying to get back to the essay and finding that piece of paper and thinking about…stuff…It's all reptile brain activity and you know it's bad, but…

If you're a Psychology student, you may recognise it's an absolutely classic case of intermittent reinforcement. If you do something frequently enough, *occasionally* something good happens, and that's enough to make you think the behaviour is worth repeating. So, you keep looking at Facebook, and every now and then something good happens, so you keep doing it, and doing it, and doing it…

Really, you're a pigeon in a box with levers and a food trough (Oh, go look it up…Skinner).

> **Eight ways to get slightly offline**
>
> 1. *Switch off (permanently) alerts* for Facebook and texting and Twitter. Easily done.
> 2. *Switch off the Internet connection* (temporarily); make a written note of the questions and queries you have in working whilst not connected.
> 3. *Get a dirt-cheap ratty old second-hand computer* with no modem, and use it for typing up essays—so you're not tempted to just quickly check Facebook…
> 4. *Give your phone to your parents* and ask them to give it back once you show them the finished work (but set a pass-code or they might read your messages…).
> 5. *Know how much time you spend online doing stupid things*—get something like TimeSnapper, which shows you how much time you spend on different sites—ouch.
> 6. *Get an app.* Ironic or what? But those apps like 'self control' or the Facebook blockers—they may work for you.
> 7. *Work without a computer*—leave your bag and computer, just use pen and paper and plan your ideas. Doubly useful as practice for exams.
> 8. *Work somewhere else*—take that pen and paper and work in the guest room, the dining room, an empty classroom after school, a public library…

The One Month Crash Crisis Revision Course

I hate to write this, but I know from bitter experience that revision is the last thing students think about and then too late. *But if you read the rest of this book, you won't need to read this section.*

You know you should have started revising months ago, but you didn't and maybe you couldn't. And now it's Spring Break and you're in meltdown. Here's the absolutely stripped down, dumbed down, heaven help you, crash course in two pages.

The absolutely unavoidable things to start with

However bad the crisis may feel, you still *have* to take a couple of hours to catch up with three things. Just panicking and starting to read textbooks is going to waste precious energy and time. Three things you must know:

1. You have to know exactly *what* to revise.
2. You have to *organise* your time.
3. You have to know a few tricks of *how* to revise.

Knowing what to revise

Make a list of all your topics per subject on a sheet of paper, something you can see in one look. Just a word or phrase to describe each topic is fine.

You can do this quickly with an OSC Revision Guide, or maybe with one of the proposed IB Guides.

If you don't want to buy revision guides, then get copies of your Subject Guide / Syllabus from your teacher and mark what you need to study.

Organising your time

Get a calendar or wall planner, as big as you can find, that covers April and May. Even better if you can divide each day into three sections. Each one represents a potential revision session.

Write in your exams timetable in May, each exam paper in one of those three sections.

Cross out a section in every day that you know you won't work a session—days when you have trips, holidays, Friday nights (get real…), parties, dentist, etc. Cross off another section on days you still have classes. Count the total sessions that are left. Maybe 50?

Just believe me—maximum useful length of session is probably 80 minutes, plus breaks. And you probably can usefully manage three sessions of revision in a day. This is seriously true. You can spend many more hours at your desk, but it's doubtful you achieve more than making yourself feel better.

Allocate topics to sessions as best you can, even if it's just by subjects. Try and spread the subjects out across the weeks—it's more efficient use of time. Don't forget to allocate sessions between exams.

How to revise—quick tricks

You really ought to read the section on 'How to revise'. But you probably won't. So, here's the most useful summary from that section of what to do. Some of these things below you can obviously do by yourself, but you're going to find it *much* more efficient to work with one or more other people—ask around and see who else needs to work as hard as you.

Big Author's Tip

Get a Revision Guide for each of your subjects from OSC at

osc-ib.com.

If you order online, they dispatch very quickly. These help you know what you need to study, and help you organise your time.

Awkward declaration of interest: this is an OSC book. Oops.

Author's Tip

You can download a personalised exam timetable from osc-ib.com or get a general timetable from ibo.org

Ten great ways to revise (with work mates)

1. Make note cards to share (see 'Memory').
2. Explain concepts to each other.
3. Summarise Subject (Examiners') Reports.
4. Get past papers to look at; do 'outline' answers.
5. Identify problems you both / all have, to ask teachers about.
6. Write summary posters of units / topics on a big piece of paper.
7. Test each other on the definitions in science syllabuses.
8. Write Post-its to put round your house.
9. Learn two quotations per exam text per 80 minute study session.
10. Test each other on understanding the Assessment Criteria.

⊗ *Don't* just re-read your notes and textbooks—it's an almost complete waste of time. You have to do something to the information to remember it.

⊗ *Don't* work too late at night—you think you're working but you actually learn very slowly; recall rates are useless, and you micro-sleep.

⊘ *Do* try reading the sections in this book on how to revise, and how your memories work—they may actually be worth an hour.

Making Money from the IB

What a surprise. Really. How did I know this would be one of the first sections you would look at?

Obviously, because you don't usually put 'exams' and 'moneymaking' together, but maybe you should. Exams are a multi-billion (yes, *multi-billion*) dollar industry, and a lot of people make a lot of money out of them. (There's a hilarious insider's description of how the testing industry in the USA works in *Making the Grades* by Todd Farley.) (And here's a great research project: find out what the IBO's budget is, and roughly how it's spent—tell me what you find out.) So, why shouldn't you make a little bit?

And indeed, why shouldn't I? That's why the dozen tips on how to make money are buried throughout this book, and you need to *buy the book* to find them. How to make money from tutoring, from exam papers, from summaries, your notes, from improved handwriting, and solved spelling problems. But they *are* there, and the book is cheap. So, just buy the book. Thanks.

More Reading...More?

These are not strictly references, although I have found many of these useful. I find it very, very hard to pay hard-earned money for books, unless they're excellent. Nor do I shop-lift. So this is a list of books that, in my opinion, are worth paying money for, and mostly quite enjoyable to read.

Presentations

Lend Me Your Ears (London: Vermilion, 2004), by M. Atkinson. An excellent book on how to organise and present ideas, from a professional consultant to politicians.

CAS and service

365 Ways to Change the World (London: Myriad Editions: 2008), by M. Norton. A different activity for each day of a year, of things you can actually do. Absolutely brilliant.

Managing your teacher

Getting to Yes, by A. Fisher and W. Ury (London: Random House, 1999). A short but outstanding guide to negotiating by a couple of Harvard academics. Everything from getting a better price on buying an iPhone, to the Middle East peace process.

Handwriting

Better Handwriting (Abingdon: Teach Yourself, 2010), by R. Sassoon and G. S. E. Briem. Teach Yourself Series. If you've got the motivation, this is a very good practical guide from start to finish.

Memory

Your Memory: A User's Guide (London: Carlton Books, 2004), by A. D. Baddeley...Aging slightly, but a great tour of many aspects of memory with lots of great stories. Very good source for TOK presentations...

Sleep

Counting Sheep (London: Flamingo 2003), by Paul Martin. An excellent and entertaining guide to everything you are likely to want to know about sleep, insomnia, what happens if you don't sleep, whether flies dream...

Tests-the truth

Making the Grade (Oakland: Berret-Koehler, 2009), by T. Farley. An awful, unbelievable but true, hilarious account of how they run the mammoth High School tests in the USA. *Almost* enough to make you glad you're doing IB...

Your Brain

Why Men Don't Listen and Women Can't Read Maps (London: Orion, 2001), by A. Pease and B. Pease. Not heavy-duty academic, but it is an extremely entertaining (and thought-provoking) survey of brain function, with particular attention to gender differences, e.g., why men have side-on car accidents and women head-on accidents.

Revision Guides

The OSC series—over 50 books designed to help you with the revision process in different IB subjects, written by experienced teachers / examiners.

Calendars and planning

www.osc-ib.com

OSC produce calendars for the academic year, or for the revision period only. You can get a stylish copy by asking them directly, or download free and print for yourself.

Malpractice

http://handbooks.ibo.org/exist/rest/app/pub

This is the guide to what the IBO defines as naughty behaviour and how you can seriously mess up your entire life by cheating to get maybe one point.

"One always tends to overpraise a long book simply because one has got through it."

E .M. Forster

NOTES

IBDP REVISION COURSES

Summary

Who are they for?
Students about to take their final IBDP exams (May or November)

Locations include:
Oxford, UK
Rome, Italy
Brussels, Belgium
Dubai, UAE
Adelaide, Sydney & Melbourne, AUS
Munich, Germany

Duration
2.5 days per subject
Students can take multiple subjects

The most successful IB revision courses worldwide

Highly-experienced IB teachers and examiners

Every class is tailored to the needs of that particular group of students

Features

- Classes grouped by grade (UK)
- Exam skills and techniques – typical traps identified
- Exam practice
- Pre-course online questionnaire to identify problem areas
- Small groups of 8–10 students
- 24-hour pastoral care.

Revising for the final IB exams without expert guidance is tough. Students attending OSC Revision Courses get more work done in a shorter time than they could possibly have imagined.

With a different teacher, who is confident in their subject and uses their experience and expertise to explain new approaches and exam techniques, students rapidly improve their understanding. OSC's teaching team consists of examiners and teachers with years of experience – they have the knowledge and skills students need to get top grades.

The size of our Oxford course gives some particular advantages to students. With over 1,000 students and 300 classes, we can group students by grade – enabling them to go at a pace that suits them.

Students work hard, make friends and leave OSC feeling invigorated and confident about their final exams.

We understand the needs of IBDP students – our decades of experience, hand-picked teachers and intense atmosphere can improve your grades.

"I got 40 points overall, two points up from my prediction of 38, and up 7 points from what I had been scoring in my mocks over the years, before coming to OSC. Thank you so much for all your help!

OSC Student

Please note that locations and course features are subject to change - please check our website for up-to-date details.

Find out more: 🏠 osc-ib.com/revision 📱 +44 (0)1865 512802

MID IBDP SUMMER PROGRAMMES

Summary

Who is it for?
For students entering their final year of the IB Diploma Programme

Locations include:
Harvard and MIT, USA
Cambridge, UK

Duration
Min. 1 week, max. 6 weeks
1 or 2 IB subjects per week

- Improve confidence and grades
- Highly-experienced IB teachers and examiners
- Tailored classes to meet students' needs
- Wide range of available subjects
- Safe accommodation and 24-hour pastoral care

Features

- Morning teaching in chosen IB subject
- 2nd IB subject afternoon classes
- IB Skills afternoon classes
- One-to-one Extended Essay Advice, Private Tuition and University Guidance options
- Small classes
- Daily homework
- Unique IB university fair
- Class reports for parents
- Full social programme.

By the end of their first year, students understand the stimulating and challenging nature of the IB Diploma.

They also know that the second year is crucial in securing the required grades to get into their dream college or university.

This course helps students to avoid a 'summer dip' by using their time effectively. With highly-experienced IB teachers, we consolidate a student's year one

learning, close knowledge gaps, and introduce some year two material.

In a relaxed environment, students develop academically through practice revision and review. They are taught new skills, techniques, and perspectives – giving a real boost to their grades. This gives students an enormous amount of confidence and drive for their second year.

The whole experience was incredible. The university setting was inspiring, the friends I made, and the teaching was first-class. I feel so much more confident in myself and in my subject.

OSC Student ← very true (speaking from experience)

Please note that locations and course features are subject to change - please check our website for up-to-date details.

Find out more: ⌂ osc-ib.com/mid ☎ +44 (0)1865 512802